IMAGES
of America

EARLY TUCSON

Standing in a row, and probably ready to eat, patrons and a canine pal (name unknown) were photographed with the cook in front of the downtown Palace Hotel Restaurant. Their serious expressions belie the February 19, 1880, enthusiastic endorsement by the *Arizona Weekly Star* that "no better table is set this side of San Francisco." (AHS B109346.)

ON THE COVER: After a contentious debate on whether or not to pave Congress Street, with opponents proclaiming that horses would slip and fall on a slick surface, Tucson narrowly voted to begin paving in 1912. Pictured *c.* 1920, city workers pave east of Scott Avenue near two long-established businesses, Kitt's and Sons, which dealt in dry goods and men's furnishings, and the Kress Company, famous for selling notions. (AHS B32475.)

IMAGES
of America

EARLY TUCSON

Anne I. Woosley and
the Arizona Historical Society

Arizona Historical Foundation

ARCADIA
PUBLISHING

Published by Arcadia Publishing
Charleston, South Carolina

Library of Congress Catalog Card Number: 2008924288

For all general information contact Arcadia Publishing at:
Telephone 843-853-2070
Fax 843-853-0044
E-mail sales@arcadiapublishing.com
For customer service and orders:
Toll-Free 1-888-313-2665

Visit us on the Internet at www.arcadiapublishing.com

For Allan
. . . *rodeados por mil recuerdos.*

CONTENTS

ACKNOWLEDGMENTS

Telling the early history of Tucson through photographs and maps was made possible by the extensive library and archival collections of the Arizona Historical Society (AHS). All images in this volume are maintained by the Department of Library and Archives of the Southern Division in Tucson. To the donors and curators who accumulated these impressive collections for almost 150 years, and who continue to do so today, we owe our thanks. They are responsible for preserving Tucson history, a history that continues to unfold with each passing day.

Numerous individuals lent a hand in facilitating this project, and working with the historical society staff was a gratifying experience. My special appreciation goes to Kim Frontz, archivist, whose deep knowledge of the collections and love of tracking down obscure facts and photographs was invaluable. Archivists Chrystal Carpenter Burke, Jill McCleary, and Dave Tackenberg, and librarian Debbie Newman gave patiently and freely of their time to make my review of thousands of photographs possible. It would be difficult to find a more obliging and experienced media specialist than Robert Orser, who never once blinked when I requested yet another image.

For helpful conversations with fellow history enthusiasts, I thank Jim Turner, AHS community outreach; Daniel Chambers; Charlie Herner; and Jim Ayers. The friendly assistance and knowledge of collections curator Laraine Daly Jones and library volunteer Arnold Franks are gratefully recognized.

I am indebted to Bill Ponder, AHS chief administrative officer, and Deborah Ortiz, AHS executive assistant, for generously giving me the time and confidence to concentrate on this volume while the business of the Arizona Historical Society continued uninterruptedly. Deborah Shelton, Southern Division director, and Kate Reeve, library and archives head, were gracious in their consistent encouragement.

Jared Jackson, southwest acquisitions editor, and Christine Talbot, western publishing manager, both of Arcadia Publishing, were always available to answer questions or offer advice.

Finally, my profound thanks go to Allan McIntyre, my staunchest supporter and most rigorous commentator, for his role in bringing the volume to conclusion.

INTRODUCTION

Tucson's story begins thousands of years ago. Archaeological investigations unearthed traces of prehistoric people who hunted game and gathered plants throughout the Santa Cruz River Valley that date back many millennia. One village, S-cuk son (variously spelled Chuk son, Shookson, and Stjukshon), an O'odham name meaning "at the foot of black mountain," later gave its name to the town of Tucson.

The transformation of a small O'odham village into Tucson began modestly with the early 1690s explorations of the Jesuit father Eusebio Kino. The first European to contact O'odham villages along the Santa Cruz River, Father Kino established *visitas*, or mission outposts, and mapped a trail for future travelers. While Catholic priests were committed to assimilating native peoples into the church and Spanish culture, the soldiers and colonists who followed concentrated their efforts on conquering lands and becoming prosperous.

In the century after Father Kino, as Spain continued to increase its material wealth, a series of missions and presidios was constructed along the strategic northern route out of Sonora to secure new territories and encourage colonization, cattle ranching, and mining ventures. The frontier was perilous, with too few soldiers and little resources to protect colonists or their enterprises. As conditions continued to deteriorate, Col. Hugo O'Conor was assigned the task of assessing Spain's northern defenses. In 1775, Colonel O'Conor recommended a site near the village of S-cuk son and established the Presidio de San Agustin del Tucson for the Spanish crown. Most northerly of all garrisons, the presidio was charged with quelling so-called hostiles (mainly Apache), maintaining the Sonoran trade route, and founding a permanent community. The Spanish foothold, initially tenuous and much harassed by Apache raiding, was stabilized after a massive presidio wall was completed in 1782. With relative security, a mission complex, including gardens, was constructed across the river from the presidio, followed by a *convento*, or an administrative center, started in 1800.

The seeming prosperity and growth disguised a faltering once-powerful Spanish Empire, as its various colonies began to break away. Mexico revolted in 1810, gaining its independence in 1821, but the cost was high. Once again, Tucson, now the sole northernmost Mexican settlement and increasingly isolated, suffered as soldiers were pulled southward. With a lack of goods flowing north from Sonora and a sparse military presence, the Apache accelerated their attacks, agriculture and ranching diminished, and Tucson's population dwindled.

Tucson was not destined to remain part of Mexico for long in the American political climate of Manifest Destiny that looked to a Union stretching from sea to shining sea, controlling an east-west railway corridor, and securing a route to California gold fields. The Treaty of Guadalupe Hidalgo, which ended the Mexican-American War, ceded a vast region from Texas to California in 1848, and the Gadsden Purchase added nearly another 30,000 square miles. By 1854, Tucson, at least in name, was an American town, although it showed no signs of the mature community it would become. Demonstrating little law and order, and lumped with New Mexico, the nearest courts were in Santa Fe. All documents, including property ownership records, were removed or destroyed with the departure of Mexican jurisdiction. Indian warfare, especially with the Apache, who saw their existence imperiled, was a constant threat. Nevertheless, Tucson was the only settlement between El Paso, Texas, and Yuma, and all transport—whether people, goods, or mail—passed through the town.

With the onset of the Civil War in 1861 and complete military abandonment of southern Arizona as Union troops were pulled east, Apache raiding intensified. Already frustrated with the federal government, Tucson was strongly sympathetic to the Confederacy, but the entrance of the California Volunteers, under the command of Gen. James H. Carleton in 1862, quickly restored federal jurisdiction. Arizona received official territorial status in 1863, and Tucson became the seat of Pima County in 1864. Tucson served as the territorial capital from 1867 to 1877. Slowly, the village on the Santa Cruz River grew, as census data documents a population of 670 residents in 1860, 1,568 in 1864, and 3,224 in 1870. The years from 1860 to the mid-1880s witnessed frequent, bloody confrontations between the Apache and newcomers. While this was the last stand for the Apache, culminating in their subjugation, relocation, or expulsion, Tucson matured, cultivating the institutions of a settled community characterized by laws and courts, schools, churches, hospitals, a historical society, and a library.

The coming of the railroad in 1880, if not the greatest event in Tucson history, was certainly a momentous milestone. Isolation from the outside world, arduous travel, limited goods, and expensive shipping were things of the past. Professional people, including doctors, teachers, and lawyers, began to arrive. Chinese workers barred from railroad jobs established laundries, restaurants, and grocery stores. The territorial university came to town. Flat-roofed adobe structures gave way to brick, stone, and peaked roofs. Patriotism ran high as Tucsonans lobbied for statehood.

Tucson came of age after the turn of the 20th century. Change, which had accelerated with the railroad, snowballed from 1900 to 1929. Technology played a large role, as automobiles replaced horse-drawn vehicles. Automobiles, streetcars, and paved roads, combined with municipal services such as electricity, running water, and gas works, expanded neighborhoods farther from the central business district. Civic leaders aggressively marketed Tucson's mild climate and clean air to health seekers and tourists. Fine hotels, guest ranches, and motor courts accommodated winter visitors who were enticed by special attractions like the Rodeo. Businesses such as Steinfeld's and Jacome's, the promotional Sunshine Climate Club, the aviation industry, and the municipal airport flourished. Statehood was finally achieved on February 14, 1912, and although sobered by world war, the youthful city generally prospered.

With the stock market crash of 1929 and the resulting Great Depression, Tucson was a study of contrasts, of prosperity and want. Still a favorite of wealthy eastern visitors, its fashionable resorts and exclusive private schools modeled on guest ranches continued to thrive. The average citizen confronted a different reality as mining, agriculture, and construction jobs disappeared, banks closed, small businesses folded, cash flow was minimal, and 10 percent of the population became unemployed. Federal assistance programs generated jobs, and local charitable organizations rallied to provide assistance for the needy. Strong civic commitment, both private and public, saw Tucson through these difficult years.

On the eve of Pearl Harbor, December 6, 1941, Tucson was no longer the isolated village of 75 years earlier. Firmly connected to the outside world by technology, the city of 40,000 residents geared up for World War II with purpose and resolve. Quietly and hidden in the commotion of preparing for war, Tucsonans might have heard the long-ago prayers of Father Kino for the success of a community along a river in the Santa Cruz Valley.

One

A RIVER THROUGH TIME

The lush Santa Cruz Valley, watered by the Santa Cruz River, sustained O'odham farmers and the hunter-gatherers who preceded them for thousands of years. The river, together with the surrounding Sonoran desert and mountains, provided a bounty of plants and animals to feed the people. The qualities that drew indigenous people were those that attracted Irish-born Hugo O'Conor, charged by the king of Spain with the responsibility of establishing a site for the northernmost presidio of the Spanish Empire. On August 20, 1775, (here transcribed, translated, and presented as written), O'Conor wrote of the new Tucson Presidio:

> I, Hugo Oconor, knight of the order of Calatrava, colonel of infantry in His Majesty's armies and Commandant Inspector of the frontier posts of New Spain, Certify: that having conducted the exploration prescribed in Article Three of the New Royal Regulation of Presidios issued by His Majesty on the Tenth of September of 1772 for the moving of the Company of San Ignaciode Tubac in the Province of Sonora, I selected and marked out in the presence of Father Francisco Garces and Lieutenant Juan de Carmona a place known as San Agustin del Tucson as the new site of the Presidio. It is situated at a distance of eighteen leagues from Tubac, fulfills the requirements of water, pasture, and wood, and effectively closes the Apache Frontier. The designation of the new presidio becomes official with the signatures of myself, Father Francisco Garces, and Lieutenant Juan Carmona, at this Mission of San Xavier del Bac, on this Twentieth Day of August of the Year 1775.

More than two centuries ago, Spanish soldiers came to this place called Tucson, enticed by the promise of wealth and land. Generations of opportunity seekers followed and, in the process, transformed a frontier outpost.

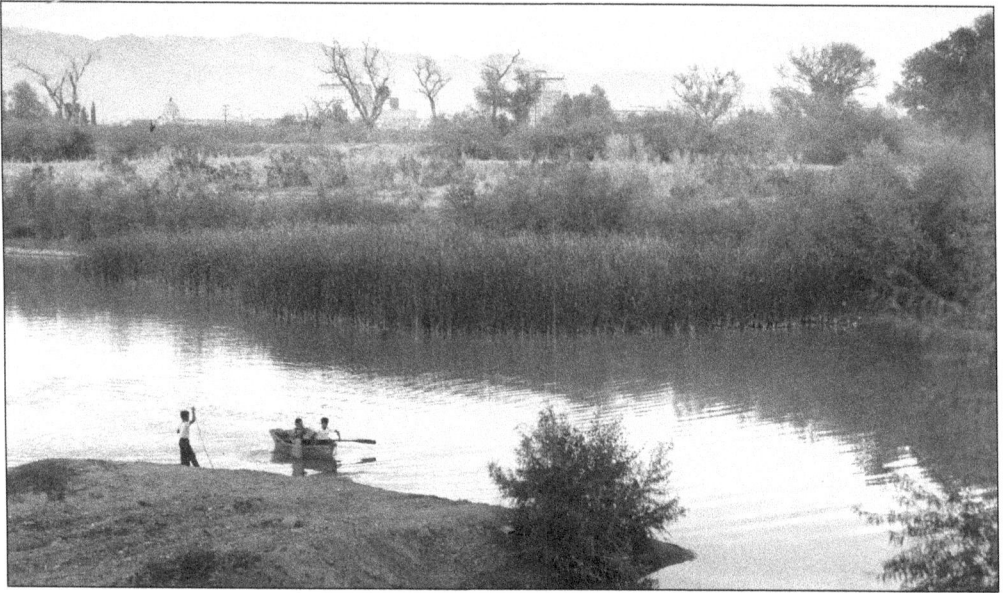

An oasis in the desert, the Santa Cruz River once created a rich habitat that sustained people for countless generations. The 1954 photograph above of pooling surface water after a summer storm is reminiscent of a scene familiar to the O'odham, Spanish explorers, and early settlers, before modern usage eliminated the permanently flowing river. In the top center, the Pioneer Hotel is flanked by the dome of the Pima County Court House on the left and the Valley Bank Building to the right. The Sonoran desert pictured below, dominated by majestic saguaro cacti, contrasts sharply against the rugged Catalina Mountains. Tucson's indigenous people were intimately familiar with the desert's plant and animal bounty that provided much of their food, including cholla buds, the fruit and pads of prickly pear, and the seeds of many grasses, as well as rabbits, pack rats, and insects. (AHS MS1255 F143-S, BN204962.)

Near Tucson only a few streams provided water and the ingredients for a prehistoric hunter or historic settler's cook pot in an otherwise arid environment. Cottonwood, ash, and willow grew along the riparian margins, creating shelter for deer, rabbits, quail, and other creatures. Seen here, Sabino Creek continues to be a favorite spot for Tucsonans. Thimble Peak in the center far view is a local landmark that is well known to hikers. (AHS PC180F282 598.)

Above, an archaeological reconstruction of a prehistoric village presents life along the Santa Cruz River as it might have occurred over a 4,000-year period. To the left, a hunter returns with a rabbit while women grind meal, winnow seeds, and place meat on a drying rack. Some make tools. Others clear a ditch irrigating their maize crop. Food is put in a storage pit for later consumption. Pots and baskets are scattered about, ready for use. Everyone is busy with the tasks of making a living. Bedrock mortars (at left) dot the rocky slopes surrounding Tucson where desert dwellers harvested wild plants. Hard-coated seeds such as mesquite beans were crushed in grinding holes, and the chaff was then winnowed to separate out the edible portion. (AHS exhibit mural, 52614.)

If not for cotton clothing and metal containers, this 1885 photograph of an O'odham family could represent the home of Tucson's prehistoric residents. Houses were dug into a shallow pit in the desert floor and covered by brush. Pottery jars for cooking and storing water, even the family dog, would have been part of desert life 2,000 years earlier. (AHS B200259.)

An O'odham woman holds her child, posing near a hammock-like crib suspended from their ramada. Made from saguaro ribs, ramadas provided relief from the desert sun. It, like the large water olla, or jar, covered with a basket (right), symbolizes a traditional way of living, while the kerosene lantern (behind the child's head) and the overturned metal washbasin (atop the ramada) reflect Euro-American influences. (AHS 57510.)

13

Gathering wood to fuel cooking fires, to build frames for houses, or to warm people on cold desert nights was an important job. Gathering wood, like filling water jars, probably needed to be done on a daily basis. An O'odham woman identified in the Arizona Historical Society archives as Felicitas Eusebio shoulders a load of wood in her carrying basket. (AHS 57557.)

Presidios functioned as garrisons that established and protected land claimed for the Spanish crown. The most northerly outpost on an unsettled frontier, San Agustin del Tucson was founded in 1775 but was not fully fortified until 1782, following repeated Apache attacks. The nucleus that promoted permanent settlements, presidios maintained routes along which people and commerce traveled. Following independence from Spain in 1821, Mexico attempted to preserve presidios with mixed success. In the reconstruction above, the Tucson Presidio's main gate (on the right) was located at the approximate intersection of today's Alameda and Main Streets. Sentinel Peak ("A" Mountain) rises in the background. The map below, probably originally drawn by Fr. Pedro Font in 1777, traces the line of presidios and missions from Sonora, Arizona, and California. It is one of the earliest citations of Tucson (here spelled Tuquison). (AHS museum diorama, G4300-F6.)

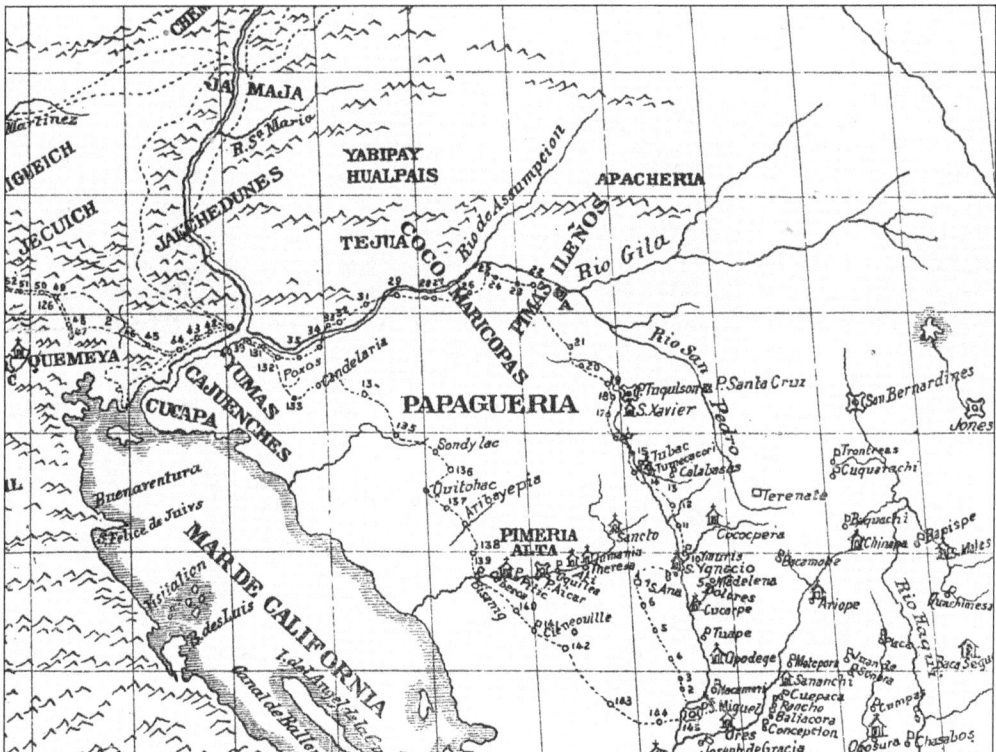

A c. 1796 map identifying Tucson's location was the result of a reconnaissance made by Fr. Diego Miguel Bringas, who was sent to assess the missions and military strength of the north. Father Bringas traveled from Sonora around 1795, stopping at missions and presidios along the way until he reached Tucson. Capt. Jose de Zuniga, commander of the troops at the presidio, provided a military escort and a translator, Pedro Rios, for Bringas's continuing journey to the Indian villages on the Gila River. Bringas produced a report and a map that are discussed in depth by Daniel Matson and Bernard Fontana. The map locates permanent, peaceful O'odham villages, as well as Spanish communities. He identifies San Agustin del Tucson as the terminal point of Christian pueblos at 32.5 degrees longitude. The Pueblo of Tucson, located on the west bank of the Santa Cruz River, probably describes an O'odham village and Spanish Catholic visita. It is separated from the Presidio of Tucson to the east. (AHS G4420-B7.)

Mission San Xavier del Bac is symbolic of the once-powerful presence of Spain in its quest for new territories and wealth in Arizona. Its founding is traditionally attributed to Fr. Eusebio Kino around 1700, but San Xavier was not completed until 1797, in the waning years of the Spanish Empire and a scant quarter century before Mexico declared its independence. The photograph is a c. 1880 stereoview by Charles Fariot, who sold his "Arizona Views" from his brother-in-law's studio in San Francisco. (AHS 9919.)

Missions were mechanisms for transforming locals into productive citizens of Spain. San Xavier's elaborate and baroque altar piece was intended to awe the senses, overwhelming worshippers by its sheer grandeur. In a time when few could read, the tenets of Catholic faith central to assimilating indigenous cultures were illustrated in color and gilt, sculpture, carving, and mural. (AHS 20728.)

17

When J. Ross Browne toured Arizona in 1864, he did not have much good to say about Tucson. His impression of San Xavier del Bac was quite the contrary when he enthused: "This is one of the most beautiful and picturesque edifices of the kind to be found on the North American continent. I was surprised to see such a splendid monument of civilization in the wilds of Arizona." His "sketch" shows the walled entry that collapsed in the 1887 earthquake, as well as Tohono O'odham houses. He noted that 200 to 300 "Papago" (that is, O'odham) souls were living around the church. Mary Ellen Fahs, Browne's great-great-granddaughter, provided a photograph of his painting for the Arizona Historical Society archives. The image depicts a visit by Col. M. O. Davidson and party to the mission complex. Davidson, a mining engineer near Arivaca, was made a special agent of the "Papago Agency" in 1864. An American flag and a gentleman waving his arms stand atop the east tower. (AHS 101060.)

The Spanish constructed San Agustin mission around 1772, later adding a *convento*, or residence, for local and visiting clergy in 1800, between Sentinel Peak and the river. Not much is known of the *convento*, but Father Iturralde, who visited on September 25, 1797, noted, "After celebrating . . . Mass at which most of the Indians attended, they said their prayers and catechism in Castilian and in Pima . . . they knew how to pray." Above, c. 1875, the impressive multistory *convento* ruins were photographed by Henry Buehman. Locals and tourists enjoyed exploring and having their pictures taken at the ruins. A 1901 pleasure party (right), identified as Myrtle Drachman and friends, has climbed onto the upper story. With the erosion of the last stub wall in 1976, the *convento* vanished altogether, ignominiously disappearing under the site of a landfill. (AHS 102106, 24447.)

After Mexico gained its independence in 1821 and expelled Spanish loyalists, Tucson became more isolated than ever, a distant outpost far from its capitol. With the virtual abandonment of the presidio and its protection, Apache raiding escalated, harvests were threatened, cattle ranching declined, and many settlers left. Tucson was an impoverished village. The adobe houses in the photograph above, c. 1890s, and the woman washing clothes in the river below depict life typical of Tucson in decades earlier. Although its circumstances were reduced, the village by the Santa Cruz River survived and was on the verge of great change. (AHS 61558, 18900.)

Two

TUCSON ON THE AMERICAN FRONTIER

After the United States gained lands following the Mexican-American War and the Gadsden Purchase, Americans moved into Tucson. Some of the first arrivals included military contingents and surveyors sent to define a new international boundary and chart a southern railway route. Others were transients on their way to somewhere else, especially the gold fields of California. Tucson became a desert stop on the southern east-to-west cross-country route along which troops, goods, mail, and people traveled. Those with an entrepreneurial spirit came—the suppliers of military posts, miners, opportunists, and business people of various kinds. Pioneers of the 1850s like Samuel Hughes, Solomon Warner, William Oury, and Charles H. Meyer would become Tucson's future civic leaders.

Although part of the United States but not yet a territory, mid-19th-century Tucson looked, felt, and sounded like a Mexican village. Tucsonans, vulnerable to what they firmly believed to be their greatest threat, the Apache, felt forgotten by the federal government as their pleas for military protection went unheeded. Consequently, most citizens declared for the Confederacy at the onset of the Civil War. Secession was short-lived as Union troops occupied the town by 1862 and established a major military supply depot.

In spite of the turbulence of the Civil and Apache Wars, the lack of justice, and the difficulty of overland travel and frontier hardships, newcomers continued to arrive. The great freighting companies of the 1860s left their indelible stamp on Tucson's development. Granted territorial status in 1863, Arizona legislators began to codify laws, establish judicial districts, create school systems, and lobby in Washington, D.C. Tucson, the capital of the Arizona Territory from 1867 to 1877, attracted pioneers, including Philip Drachman, Jacob Mansfeld, and Albert Steinfeld, who made their presence felt in the community.

Tucson during the decades from the 1850s through 1879 was a crucible in which fledgling social, judicial, and educational institutions mixed with the less salubrious realities of ethnic discrimination, lack of law enforcement, and vigilante justice. Tucson was a town on the American frontier.

John Russell Bartlett climbed Sentinel Peak on July 17 and 18, 1852, and sketched the river valley looking at Tucson in the distance below. He was impressed by the fertile land near the river "through which irritation canals ran in every direction." Bartlett mistakenly described Mission San Agustin (center right) as a "large hacienda, much decayed, but once very rich" and noted that previous extensive cultivation was greatly reduced due to Apache predations that forced people to take refuge in town. Bartlett did not admire the town, whose residents he described as "miserable," living in houses that were "hovels." Some 40 years later, Albert Reynolds photographed a growing Tucson from approximately the same location. Irrigated fields surround the mission ruins, and the Pima County Court House (left center), the Indian School (center distance), and the University of Arizona's Old Main (right distance) are visible. (AHS 917.8 B289P, PC107F56-12649.)

Tucson.

Journalist J. Ross Browne visited Tucson in 1864 and sketched the valley, town, and Catalina Mountains from Sentinel Peak. He vividly shared Bartlett's contempt for Tucson writing, "he emerges to find himself on the verge of the most wonderful scattering of human habitations his eye ever beheld—a city of mud boxes, dingy, dilapidated, cracked and baked into a composite of dust and filth." (AHS 917.91 B882t.)

Travelers from eastern cities who superimposed their preconceptions on Tucson failed to recognize that it reflected the local circumstances of a frontier town outside established routes of communication, distribution of goods, and stability. The 1870s stereoview above shows Tucson rural life adapted to its desert and cultural environment. (AHS 102304.)

23

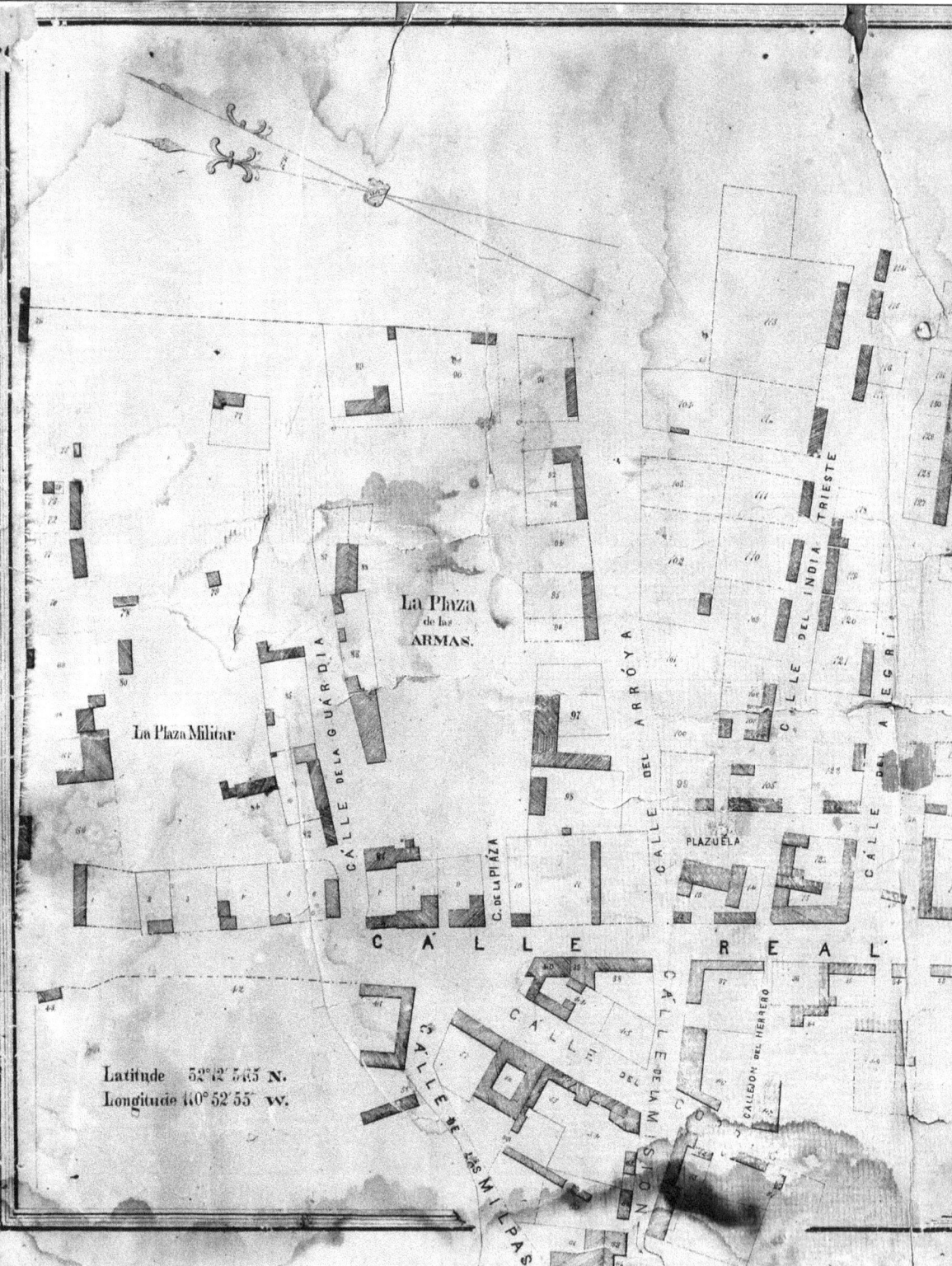

La Plaza
de las
ARMAS.

La Plaza Militar

CÁLLE DE LA GUÁRDIA

CÁLLE DEL ARRÓYA

CÁLLE DEL INDIA TRIESTE

CÁLLE DE LA ALEGRÍA

PLAZUELA

C. DE LA PLÁZA

CALLE   REAL

CALLE

CALLE DE LA MISION

CALLE DE LAS MILPAS

CALLEJON DEL HERRERO

Latitude   52°12′ 585″ N.
Longitude 110° 52′ 55″ W.

24

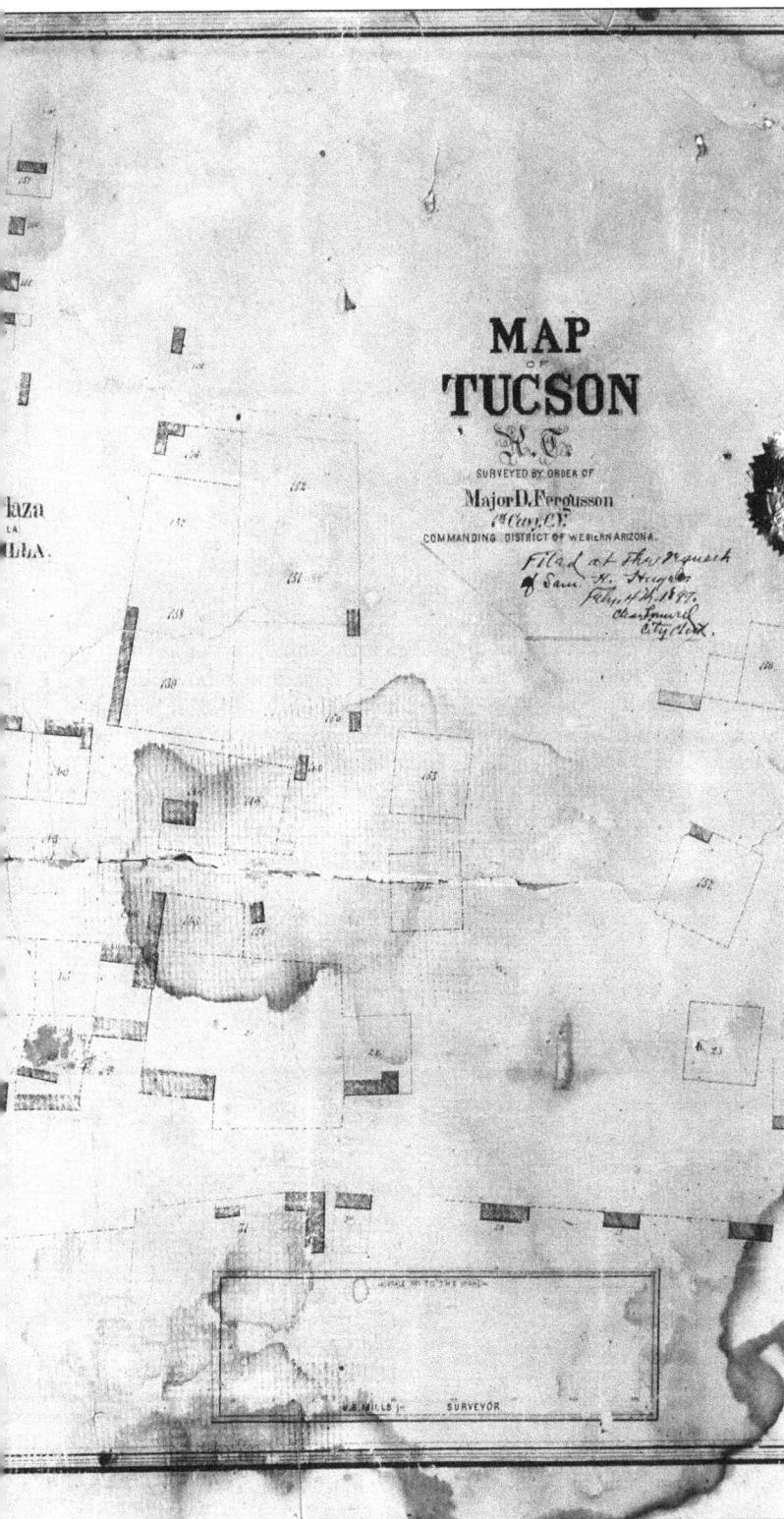

MAP
OF
TUCSON
A. T.

SURVEYED BY ORDER OF
Major D. Fergusson
1ª Cav. C.V.
COMMANDING DISTRICT OF WESTERN ARIZONA.

Filed at the request
of Sam. H. Hughes
Feby. 4th 1899.
Charles [illegible]
City Clerk.

J. B. MILLS   SURVEYOR

After the Gadsden Purchase, when Tucson came under the control of the United States, previous records were found to be removed, lost, or destroyed. Land titles were nonexistent, leaving ownership questionable. To resolve this problem, one of the first acts by Maj. David Fergusson of the First California Volunteer Cavalry and commander of the District of Western Arizona was to determine property ownership with the help of William S. Oury, Tucson's registrar. He assigned surveyor J. B. Mills to prepare a map that defined property boundaries. The so-called Fergusson Map of 1862 is Tucson's earliest street map. Precisely how it came into his possession is unclear, but Samuel Hughes filed it with the city clerk on February 4, 1899. (AHS G4334 T8 F4.)

25

Vestiges of Tucson under Spain and Mexico were incorporated into the new order as the town became increasingly "Americanized." Remains of the Spanish presidio wall (above) enclosed a yard on an alley near Alameda Street in this photograph taken on May 15, 1915, by Robert Forbes, who was appointed the dean of the University of the Arizona College of Agriculture in 1899. The second Pima County Court House tower is visible at the far right. (AHS BN92905.)

Tucson served as capital of the Arizona Territory from 1867 to 1877. Legislators conducted the business of the territory in a rented, extremely modest adobe building (here in ruins) with a dirt floor and mud roof on Ochoa Street near Stone Avenue in what was once Tucson's central business district. (AHS 632.)

The defendants of the Camp Grant Massacre on December 11, 1871, posed for their portrait in front of the first Pima County Court House, built in 1868 on the northeast corner of Church and Ott Streets. This is the earliest known photograph of any Tucson scene and, intriguingly, bears the back stamp of photographer Eadweard Muybridge. Historically, it depicts what became one of Tucson's most infamous episodes, the killing of a group of Arivaipa Apache peacefully living near Camp Grant. During 1871, hostilities with the Apache were extreme, and residents of the territory, whether Anglo, Mexican, or O'odham, believed that force, even extermination, was the only answer to peace. Prominent Tucson leaders accompanied by Mexican and O'odham men attacked the camp on Sunday, April 30, killing more than 100 Apache, mostly women and children. Public condemnation in the east demanded those involved be brought to justice and the participants tried. This was done. After a trial lasting five days, a jury of their peers acquitted more than 100 men after 19 minutes of deliberation. Judge John Titus, presiding, stands in the center. (AHS 654.)

Following the Civil War, a permanent military presence, Camp Lowell, was established in 1866 near the site of today's Santa Rita Hotel. In 1873, the post was relocated seven miles northeast of the town and renamed Fort Lowell. The fort was a supply center, escorted freighters, and served as an operational base against the Apache during the 1870s and 1880s. Considered unnecessary after the Apache wars, Fort Lowell was closed in 1891. Two images of Fort Lowell during the 1880s show the parade ground (above) looking toward Officers' Row as Charles Fearn, identified as the fort's hospital steward, leans against a mesquite tree. Officers' Row, shaded by cottonwood trees (below), gave the avenue its alternate name, Cottonwood Lane. (AHS 60400, PC208F29-F.)

Officers lived with their families at the fort. Above, a group of children were photographed in front of Lt. James B. Erwin's quarters, including his daughters Ellen (left) and Winifred (center, next to their nanny). Winifred was born at Fort Lowell in 1886. Few Tucson residents during the 1870s and 1880s had an ounce of sympathy for the Apache as a people struggling for their survival. They were viewed as savages who must be conquered if Tucson and Arizona could ever prosper. Widely distributed cabinet cards (below) depicting an Apache threatening a hapless young woman with a hatchet were typical of the day. (AHS 91618, B94655.)

The final battles between the U.S. military and the Apache occurred during the 1880s. In one instance, troops engaged the Apache at the Battle of Cibecue Creek on August 30, 1881. Believed instigated by the medicine man Nock-ay-det-klinne and his supporters, the fight included Sanchez (above), himself a band chief. Taken prisoner, Sanchez was photographed at Fort Lowell wearing a prisoner's name tag. His clothing was predominantly Anglo except for the traditional, glass trade bead necklace with a tweezers pendant (used to pluck facial and nose hair) made from a cartridge and typical Apache boots. (AHS B93784.)

At the Cibecue Creek Battle, Apache scouts attached to the army but sympathetic to Nock-ay-det-klinne changed sides, killing some soldiers. Two shackled scouts, Sergeant Dandy Jim (left) and Private Mucheco, were incarcerated at Fort Lowell and photographed on the parade ground by Henry Buehman. Attired in conventional Apache clothing, both wear prisoner tags Nos. 6 and 7. Because they were enlisted soldiers, they were treated severely. Dandy Jim was hung with two others at Fort Grant on March 3, 1882. Mucheco was given a dishonorable discharge, sent to Alcatraz, and then transferred to another federal penitentiary. He spent the rest of his life in prison at hard labor. (AHS B94656.)

Tucson celebrated the removal of Geronimo and his band on November 8, 1887, with a parade through downtown and a fete culminated by the presentation of an ornamental sword to Gen. Nelson A. Miles by Judge William H. Barnes, who extolled, "to the captain who gave peace and security to the people of Arizona." Conspicuously absent from the festivities was Lt. Charles B. Gatewood, who negotiated with and brought in Geronimo. An honor guard of members of the Society of Arizona Pioneers (later the Arizona Historical Society) carried the society banner as they passed the Opera House. The county courthouse on Pennington Street is in the distance. John Spring's adaption (below) of the Society of Arizona Pioneers banner, dated June 1, 1885, is virtually identical to the one carried in the Miles' parade (left). The banner combined icons of Tucson and the Arizona Territory. (AHS 2905, MS754.)

SAN XAVIER.

By Pioneer John A. Spring.
June 15 1885.

Defeat of the Apache deemed Fort Lowell unnecessary, and the garrison was closed in 1891. In less than 10 years, the officers' quarters showed major deterioration (above). In time, city boosters declared the ruin a must-see, and it became a major Tucson attraction. A pleasure party (below, c. 1900) jokes "hands up!" on top of J. Knox Corbett's stagecoach that he had purchased from the government. Corbett was an entrepreneur, Tucson postmaster, and mayor who transported picnickers to the old fort for a day's outing. (AHS 61561, 13797.)

Educating Tucson's youth was on the minds of community leaders even during the tumultuous 1870s. The first permanent public school was built on the corner of Congress Street and Sixth Avenue in 1875. The land and $5,000 needed for construction were donated by businessman Estevan Ochoa. At one point, parents were outraged when the principal decided to put girls and boys in the same classroom, but that tempest was temporary, and instruction continued. (AHS 25951.)

Prominent merchant E. N. Fish constructed his home at Main Avenue and Alameda Street in 1868. His house and the Congress Street School conform to the architectural style prevalent until the late 1800s, of long, flat-roofed adobe structures. Fish married Maria Wakefield, who, with Harriet Bolton, were Tucson's first women teachers. (AHS 62105-A.)

34

Until 1881, Tucson was supplied by overland routes, whether south from Mexico, west through Yuma, or east from Santa Fe. Pictured in the 1870s, a mule freight train meant that residents could expect goods ranging from sugar, darning needles, nails, and buckets, to calico and hammers. Companies such as Tully and Ochoa, Lord and Williams, and William and Louis Zeckendorf profited from army service contracts and selling to locals. (AHS 102081.)

From the days of the Spanish, the promise of gold and silver lured the adventuresome to Arizona. Eastern publications were effusive, writing how the area "is located in the heart of the extraordinary metalliferous region of the Santa Cruz Valley." Many Tucsonans speculated, but mining was hard going, as shown here at the Bushell Mine in the 1870s. More individuals probably made money by selling supplies to miners as opposed to striking it rich. (AHS 18817.)

New Yorker Charles O. Brown (right, standing with his son William) came west on the heels of the California Gold Rush. Brown's activities prior to settling permanently in Tucson were shady, possibly extending to outlawry, which was easier than panning for gold. He established the Congress Hall Saloon in 1868 and was by then a respected businessman. Legislators conducted territorial business at the saloon, and Tucson pioneers discussed forming a Society of Arizona Pioneers there. (AHS 20858.)

The earliest water-powered flour mills soon gave way to mills located more distantly from the Santa Cruz River. James Lee and William Scott built the Eagle Steam Flour Mill in 1870 on South Main Street where it intersects with Broadway Boulevard. In turn, the Scotts sold the business to E. N. Fish, who partnered with Leo Goldschmidt, who, in turn, bought out Fish's share around 1898. Renamed the Eagle Milling Company, an enlarged facility was built on Toole Avenue (above). (AHS 46696.)

Three

PRELUDE TO CHANGE

The seeds of what Tucson pioneers would have called "civilization" firmly sprouted during the latter decades of the 19th century. Although still a modest village, citizens felt a sense of security as the Apache were removed to reservations or expelled from the territory altogether. A true sense of community existed, where everyone knew everyone else. Schools were improved, and spiritual life was robust, as reflected by the number of churches. The Presbyterians and Sisters of Carondelet were strong forces among the O'odham, operating the Indian boarding school, the orphanage, and a hospital. Originally not considered much of a victory, the university came to Tucson. A library appeared on the second floor of the city hall and the Arizona Historical Society (then known as the Society of Arizona Pioneers) began to collect pioneer history. Equally active, saloons and businesses on Maiden Lane contributed to a lively downtown.

The clearest sign of progress, and one that initiated the most far-reaching changes in Tucson's history up to this point, was the arrival of the railroad in 1880. Tucson's isolation began to recede. Suddenly, rough lumber no longer cost $300 per linear board feet but was affordable. No longer was kerosene so costly that residents had to rely on smoky homemade candles. Rail connection meant greater availability, diversity, and quantity of reasonably priced goods. It also meant the increased Americanization of a community that heretofore was primarily influenced by Mexico to the south. Beginning in 1880, eastern styles permeated everything from Victorian architecture, fashion, and home furnishings, to the configuration of streets and residential neighborhoods. The railroad created new jobs and opportunities for businesses, large and small, to proliferate and prosper. Tucson became part of America and, wishing ardently for statehood, demonstrated its patriotism by fervent support of the Spanish-American War that ended the 19th century.

COMPLIMENTS

ARIZONA BONANZA

PUBLISHED BY

Buehman

TUCSON, A. T.

Noted Tucson photographer Henry Buehman opened his first studio in 1874 and quickly became an ardent civic booster, praising the natural resources of the Arizona Territory. His cabinet and stereoview cards show some of the earliest views of Tucson, the environs, and its residents. In this playful-yet-serious cabinet card, Buehman produced a collage of Tucson children he had photographed, calling it Arizona Bonanza. Dated, April 1, 1890, on the reverse Buehman declared: "No indeed: the world never produced a greater bonanza. . . . Fifty years from now some one of the boys herein represented may be called upon to occupy the Presidential chair . . . and others may lead the world in science, art and literature. Our girls may grace the White House . . . in the capacity of helpmeets . . . when they as little girls wended their way together to the same school . . . and matured in the same beneficent climate. I dedicate the work to the boys and girls of Arizona." (AHS MS1115 F137.)

Photographer Carleton Watkins captured Tucson one month in the springtime when he was sent by the Southern Pacific Railroad to photograph the area from April 10 to May 18, 1880. His images, both shot from the Palace Hotel, show a small town dominated in both business district and neighborhoods by modest, flat-roofed adobe structures. Meyer Street (above), occupied by numerous merchants, was unpaved, unlit, and had no sidewalks. Pearl Street (below), located near Main Street but now long gone, was typically domestic with a cluster of houses, outbuildings, fields, livestock, wagons, and hay. Irrigation ditches that watered fields tapped into a cottonwood tree bordered Santa Cruz River. (AHS 14841, 14839.)

Burros, a favored mode of transport, were led through a neighborhood alley behind the Park Brewery off Pennington Street, c. 1880. The second building on the right shows the rapid erosion that can occur when an adobe building is left to the elements. Below, three boys—one holding a lunch pail—probably on their way to school, stand still for photographer Willis P. Haynes on Stone Avenue just south of Congress Street. Although shown here as dusty and lacking sidewalks, the 1881 Tucson business directory nonetheless described Stone Avenue as a spacious and promising thoroughfare. (AHS B109289, AHS 18806.)

Willis Haynes portrayed Tucson life of the 1880s and revealed its Indian, Mexican American, and Euro American ethnic-cultural mix. Burros were not the only means of transport, as witnessed by the gigantic bundle of hay shouldered by the Tohono O'odham woman. Fuel and hay were much in demand by consumers. (AHS 26458.)

Meyer Street as viewed between West Seventeenth and Kennedy Streets with Dan Won and Company Groceries on the corner. The covered, sloped entrance, or *toldo*, to buildings (on right) provided protection from sun or rain. The *canales*, or drainpipes, were a necessary component to flat-roofed adobes and sudden summer monsoon rains. Electric streetlights help date the photograph to around 1883. (AHS 15578.)

The Southern Pacific Railroad rumbled into the depot (pictured above in the 1890s) on March 20, 1880, at 11:00 a.m. to a jubilant crowd. Tucson was connected to the outside world by rail for the first time. Great civic exuberance marked the occasion at Levin's Park, with numerous, lengthy speeches by dignitaries and calls for a reported 14 toasts, plus appropriate responses. Locomotives required extensive maintenance (below, c. 1888) to keep them operational. Massive steam engines were serviced in the roundhouse (center right), while blacksmiths, boilermakers, and machinists worked in nearby shops (center left). Sam Oliver's boardinghouse is the two-story building (left foreground), with his adjacent residence on the right. (AHS 18337, B200280.)

Court Plaza between Pennington and Alameda Streets illustrates Tucson's burgeoning prosperity and developing social institutions, c. 1880. The impressive two-story Presbyterian church (left) was Tucson's first protestant place of worship. Prominent businessman Barron Jacobs built a 17-room adobe mansion (center) with Victorian architectural influences. Casa Cordova (far right) is now a part of the Tucson Museum of Art. (AHS BD109345.)

Although Jewish pioneer entrepreneurs arrived in Tucson as early as the 1850s, no formal synagogue existed for another half century, and services were held in private homes. A group of Jewish women, led by Clara Ferrin Bloom and Terese Marx Ferrin, formed the Hebrew Ladies Aid Society, which was committed to filling this vacuum. The society began raising funds in 1905. Their efforts culminated with the first worship service in the first synagogue in the Arizona Territory on Rosh Hashanah eve, October 3, 1910, at Temple Emanu-El on Stone Avenue. (AHS BN23800.)

The second Pima County Court House (pictured above, *c.* 1884), a monument to High Victorian splendor, replaced its modest adobe predecessor at the corner of Church and Pennington Streets. The imposing brick-and-stone building was a clear indication that law and order was securely established in Tucson. In less than 10 years, Court Plaza (below), shaded by mature trees, became a site of local gatherings and concerts. City hall is to the left of the courthouse, the spires of San Agustin Cathedral rise in the right distance, and horse-drawn trolleys provide public transportation (foreground). A banner between the trolleys reads, Grade 8 1892. (AHS BN205699, 13401.)

Plaza School (pictured above, *c.* 1890), renamed the Safford School for Gov. Anson P. K. Safford, was completed in 1884. Located near Armory Park, many parents feared that being so far east in the open desert, their children might be vulnerable to Apache attacks. Besides instruction in literature, history, Latin, algebra, bookkeeping, and other subjects, a kindergarten and the "study of the nature of alcoholic drinks and narcotics and their effect on the human system" were introduced by 1886. From 1887 through 1888, 528 students, representing all grades, were enrolled. The instructor, identified as a Miss Barrett, posed with her students for a class picture (seen below, *c.* 1890). Compulsory attendance was legislated in 1899 for ages 8 to 14, with exemptions made for families who could not provide suitable clothing. Apparently, exceptions did not extend to shoes, as several students are without. (AHS BN202435, 26784.)

As early as 1883, the federal government asked the Presbyterian Church to open a boarding school among the "Pima Indians." The Women's Board of Home Missions organized the Tucson Indian Training School "to offer a practical Christian education to the Pima and Papago Indian youth." Classes began with 10 students in 1886 in leased facilities, but by 1887, a larger site was purchased south of Tucson, and buildings were constructed with an opening enrollment of 54 students in 1888. Students and staff gathered in front of a school building (pictured above, c. 1890). On probably the same day, women teachers were photographed with female students (shown below). Academic instruction reached the eighth-grade level, but "manual and domestic arts" such as carpentry and farming for boys, and sewing and cooking "to a civilized standard" for girls were emphasized. The school's second superintendent, Frazier Herndon, would help form the Papago Reservation in 1916. (AHS B109160, B93870.)

In an oft-told story the university and an appropriation of $25,000 was the consolation prize given Tucson by the 13th Territorial Legislature (1885) that kept the desirable capital in Prescott, awarded the profitable asylum to Phoenix, and the prison to Yuma. Nevertheless, once the deed was done, Jacob Mansfeld took a walk in the desert east of town, picked a site, and persuaded hesitant owners to donate land for the university. Ground was broken on October 27, 1887, and the doors to Old Main (pictured above) opened on October 1, 1891. At that time, Old Main was the university, with classrooms, laboratories, offices, a kitchen, mess, and temporary quarters for faculty and students. Uncommon in the 1890s, University of Arizona women medical students studied anatomy in Old Main (shown below). (AHS B200279, B109201.)

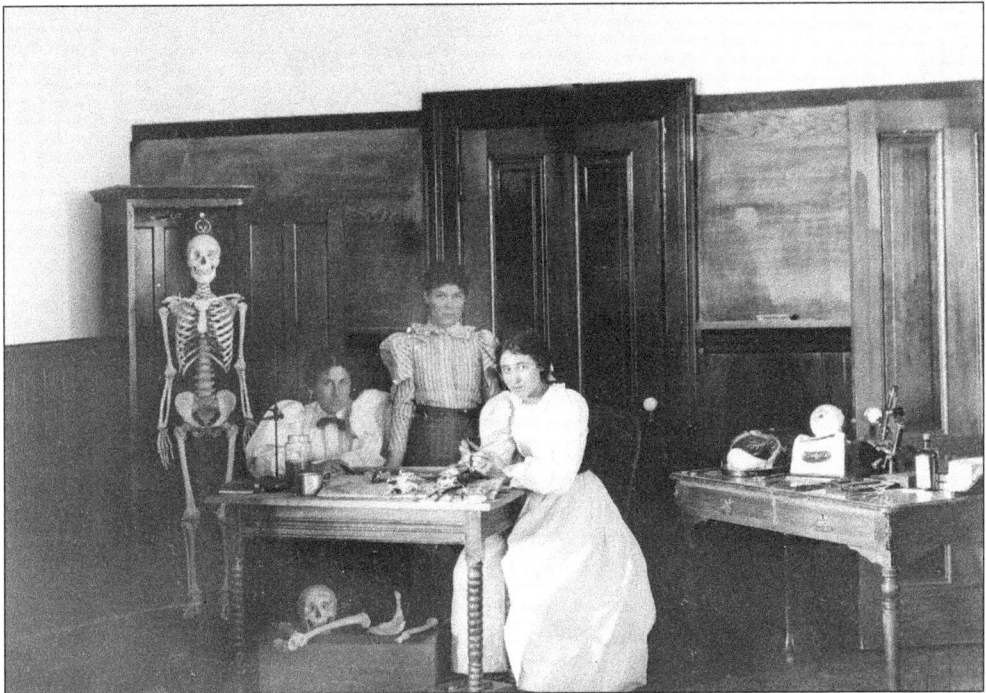

An early Tucson mover and shaker, Barron M. Jacobs, in addition to other lucrative family businesses, organized the Consolidated Bank, of which he was the first president in 1890, with the merger of several territorial banks. In 1903, the bank building at 200 West Congress Street became available and served as the home of the Arizona Pioneers Historical Society at a rent of $15 per month for 20 years. (AHS BN203763.)

Jany. 31, 1884.

THE BEGINNING OF THE SOCIETY OF ARIZONA PIONEERS.

By Sam. Hughes.

Samuel Hughes, one of Tucson's earliest pioneers, arrived in town on March 12, 1858. In his day, Hughes made and lost money as a butcher, merchandiser, miner, land speculator, and moneylender, but always had a reputation for public spiritedness. A founding member of the Society of Arizona Pioneers (later renamed the Arizona Pioneers Historical Society, and finally the Arizona Historical Society), Hughes designed a society logo that included a saguaro, Gila monster, and horned lizard, c. 1885. (AHS MS366.)

Carleton Watkins photographed the Palace Hotel in 1880, when it was said to be the fanciest building in town since its construction in 1875. Not only was the two-story, brick hotel a favorite spot for dances, its restaurant and saloon were much frequented, and the first meetings of the Arizona Pioneers Historical Society were held in a hotel clubroom. (AHS 18762.)

The Occidental Hotel on Meyer Street afforded visitors lodging from the latter 1870s and was one of Tucson's few upscale establishments in the 1880s. Pima County sheriff Charles Shibell operated both the Occidental and Palace Hotels during the early 1880s before returning to public service as the Pima County recorder. (AHS 13325.)

An old view of San Xavier Hotel, Tucson, Arizona

The increasing number of travelers brought by rail and Tucson's limited lodging facilities encouraged the Southern Pacific Railroad to build the fashionable San Xavier Hotel on Toole Avenue in 1881 (upper and lower views, c. 1890). Elegantly appointed with the finest dining, as described in the City Directory, its proximity to the tracks, wooden construction, and live sparks from locomotives did not make for a happy mix; it burned to the ground in 1903. (AHS 2871, 13322.)

Workers laid track for the Tucson Street Railway on Main Street (pictured above, c. 1899). Public transportation began as early as 1879 with horse-drawn carriages. A system of cars pulled along tracks by horses or mules, each accommodating 16 passengers, started in 1898. The white building (center right) is the Fremont House. A streetcar (shown below) traveled north on Sixth Avenue between Congress and Tenth Streets in January 1899, passing W. E. Felix, Headquarters for Gents Furnishings Goods. (AHS 74365, 13604.)

Looking west on Congress Street (pictured above, c. 1890) toward Sentinel Peak (left, behind light post) and the wedge—a row of shops that divided the west Congress business section (on the left) from Maiden Lane (on the right), Tucson's red-light district. The Radulovich block (right), with multiple shops and offices was one of Tucson's busiest. Barriers around the trees kept horses from nibbling their bark. On September 17, 1898, the block was gutted in one of the worst fires in Tucson's history. Below, smoke is still rising from the smoldering remains several days later. Merchants lost buildings and inventory, Charles Hoff's Sunset Telephone and Telegraph offices were destroyed, and University of Arizona chancellor William Herring's 1,800-volume library burned. (AHS B91385, 633.)

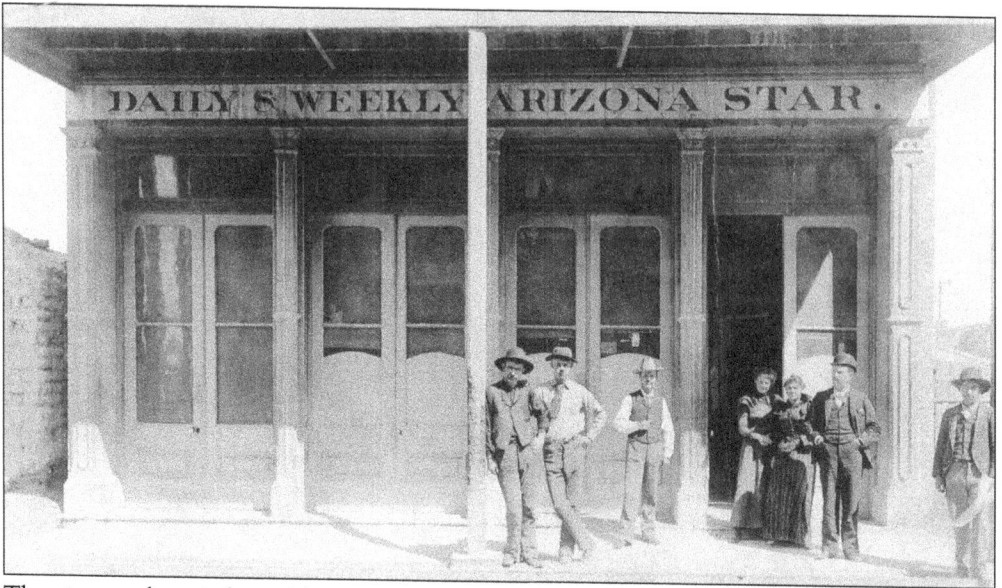

The city was kept informed by its newspapers. First founded in 1877 by Charles H. Tully and Louis C. Hughes as the *Daily Bulletin*, the *Star* progressed through a series of names, including the *Daily and Weekly Arizona Star*, with offices located on North Church Street. The presence of Robert Asa Todd (far left), who arrived in Tucson in 1893 and served as the city editor until 1896, helps date this A. S. Reynolds photograph. The name *Arizona Daily Star* became official in 2000. (AHS 13316.)

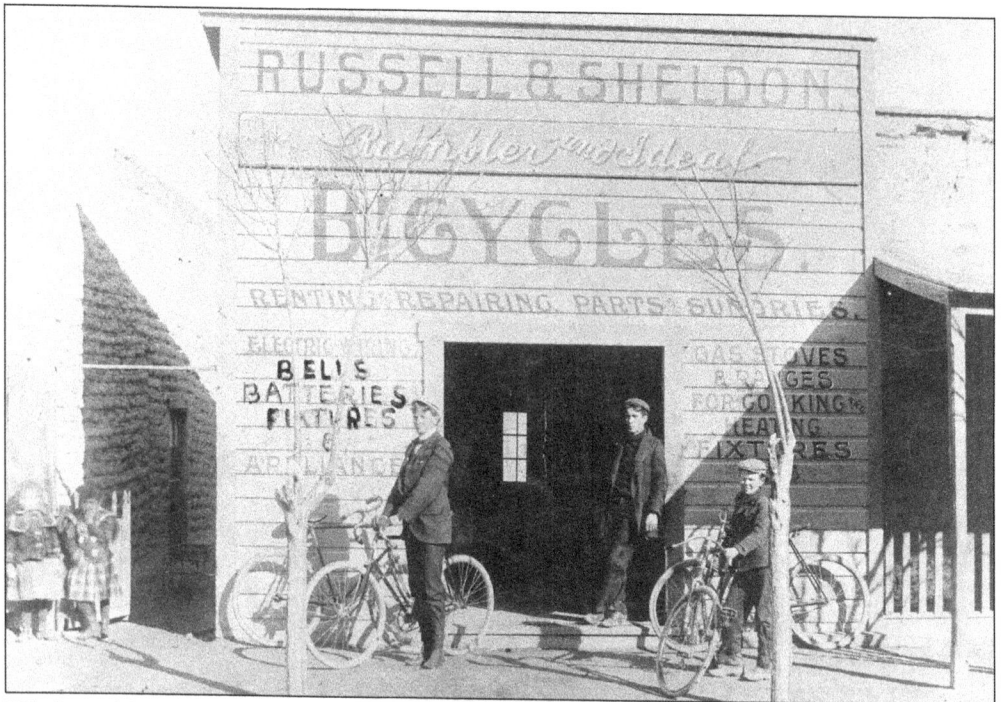

While problematical during Tucson's rainy season on unpaved streets, bicycles were a favored means of travel. Russell and Sheldon's shop on Church Street, located across from the Pima County Court House, served the needs of Tucson's many bicycle enthusiasts. (AHS 27152.)

The Chinese arrived in Arizona as laborers in mines and railroad construction. Although legislation barred them from numerous jobs by the late 1870s, many remained in Tucson, establishing groceries, laundries, and farms of their own. Wing Sing's Laundry (pictured above), located across from the railroad depot on Ninth Street, served many railroad employees and passengers of the 1890s. As is apparent from bilingual store signs, Charley Lee's Grocery (shown below, c. 1898) sold fresh produce and butter to English and Spanish customers alike. (AHS 13610, 13298.)

If residents wished to venture to Tucson's notorious Maiden Lane, they could have their shoes repaired at No. 91. The 1899–1900 Tucson City Directory lists the shop's owner as Encarnacion Salas, shoemaker. The non-sporting businesses of Maiden Lane finally began to flourish when, after long debate, the lane was incorporated into Congress Street, and its ladies were removed to Gay Alley. (AHS 13300.)

Many businesses sprung up around the railroad depot. Lunch and libations were provided at Bohn's Cactus Saloon and Lunch Counter or the Wigwam Lunch Parlor in the 1890s, where patrons could get a beer for 5¢, a variety of sandwiches, and a room for 25¢. If all the rooms were occupied, a night's sleep was available at the nearby Park Hotel, located across Toole Avenue from the depot on Fifth Avenue. (AHS 13365.)

Fleishman's and Martin's were two of Tucson's earliest pharmacies. Frederick Fleishman's drugstore (pictured above) was actually the first in the Arizona Territory, when it was established as La Botica (drugstore) by his father-in-law, Charles Meyer, in 1858. Meyer gave the store to Fleishman when he married his daughter, Carlotta, and it was renamed in 1882. George Martin opened his drugstore in 1884 at 32 Camp Street (now Broadway Boulevard) and later relocated the business to Congress and Church Streets (shown below). The Martin drugstore was the first to boast a soda fountain in 1888 and remained in the family, serving the Tucson community until 1954. Photographed in his store in 1891, George Martin stands at back left. (AHS 22137, 45169.)

Toward the end of the 19th century, the face of Tucson changed rapidly. Prior to that time, modest adobe buildings with flat roofs made of locally available materials were the norm, especially in the poorer sections of town (pictured above, *c.* 1885). Sonoran-style homes (shown below) were also constructed of adobe and had flat roofs with little or no ornamentation, although they were much more finished in appearance. The economic contrast between the families pictured here is obvious, one possibly making a living by farming and the other employed in town. The latter was photographed complete with family dolls and horse. (AHS 18692, B111384.)

MacTroy McCleary's home, shown c. 1885 at 241 West Franklin Street, was a basic Sonoran-style flat-roof structure showing definite Victorian influences, including capped posts, saw-cut porch brackets and railings, and a projecting porch. Walls were often painted or inscribed to resemble stone. The quantity of lumber used is clear evidence of a post-railroad home. McCleary (left) was photographed with Gertrude McCleary Ochoa, Carmen McCleary, and the family dog. (AHS 44266-A.)

Dr. Henry H. Pilling's residence, located at the corner of Pennington Street and North Sixth Avenue, pictured in the 1890s, reflected the new Victorian style with fancy, decorative wooden trim, a pitched roof, ornamented glass windows, and brick instead of adobe. In late-19th-century neighborhoods, the front yards of homes were enclosed by a fence and set back from the street. Dr. Pilling was a respected Tucson homeopathic physician. (AHS B91799.)

Arizona Historical Society archives contain many photographs of families posing at their residences. These images often include multiple generations living under one roof, such as the Benjamin Heney family, which included the youngest, Ben Jr., astride Oury, his Shetland pony, to the eldest, Mrs. M. G. Roca (above). Benjamin Heney, an Arizona pioneer, served as the county treasurer, tax collector, and mayor. Teddy Roosevelt offered to appoint Heney as the territorial governor, but he declined. Mariano G. Samaniego (below right, c. 1890), a businessman, founder of the Alianza Hispano-Americana, and member of the first University of Arizona Board of Regents, among other enterprises, poses with members of his family in their sunny garden with raised planting beds. (AHS PC62 54074, 57878.)

Photographs of individuals provide glimpses into the diverse cultural fabric of the community. Manuel Fimbres (pictured above) stood at his *milpa*, or garden plot, which is growing a healthy crop of corn on his property at Alameda Street, west of the Santa Cruz River, in 1895. A young Harold Steinfeld (shown below), son of Tucson pioneer and business leader Albert Steinfeld, who later became prominent himself, poses in a goat cart in 1896 at 300 North Main Avenue, the family home. (AHS 64322, PC208F17 29155.)

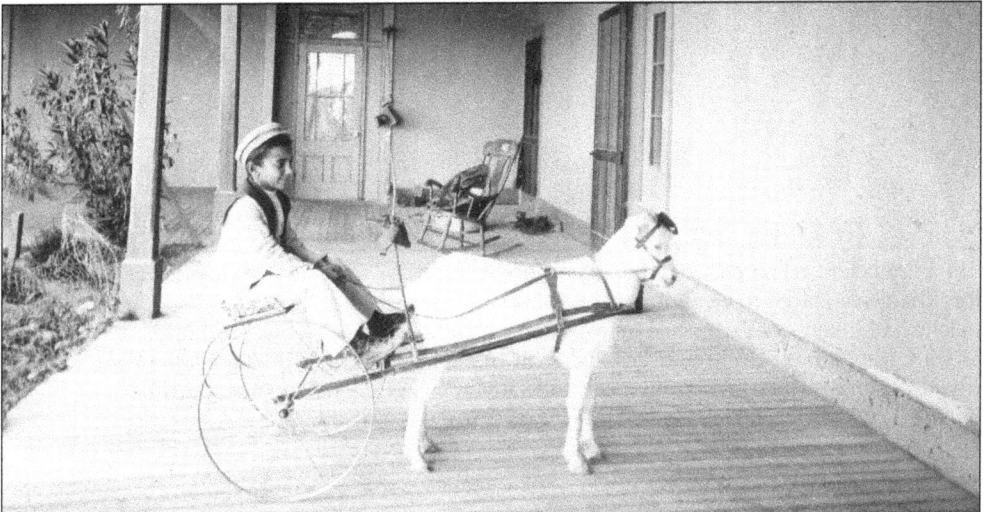

In an era before television or radio, Tucsonans found ways to entertain themselves. Excursions into the desert, often to be photographed adjacent (or in) a giant saguaro were popular. Glenton (left) and Gilbert Sykes, sons of famed scientist and designer of both the Lowell and Steward Observatory domes, Godfrey Sykes, did a bit of exploring on March 25, 1908. Glenton Sykes would become a Tucson city engineer and Gilbert Sykes a local aviator. Both became highly regarded for their deep knowledge of the natural world. (AHS PC240F47A.)

Picnics to some shady spot were a favorite Sunday pastime, especially during hot summer months. Jennie Crepin (pictured above on horseback), wife of Willis P. Haynes, and a party of friends enjoyed themselves on the banks of the Santa Cruz River, c. 1885. Tucsonans, like folks elsewhere, were avid baseball fans. The Tucson Baseball Team (shown below, c. 1890) was photographed at Fort Lowell on what probably was the abandoned parade grounds, which the team used as their field. From left to right are (seated) ? Mertz, Harry A. Drachman, J. Blinkhorn, Mose Drachman, and Walter Zabriskie; (standing) E. Hutton, Emanuel Drachman, Abe Goldbaum, B. J. Zabriskie, Frank Smith, and Dave Hughes. (AHS 18733, 2635.)

Tucsonans of the 1880s and 1890s amused themselves with musical concerts, whether an impromptu recital by family and friends featuring two guitars and two banjos (pictured above) or a street performance by the Mariner's Band in front of Sam Drachman's Cigar Company store at the wedge on Congress Street and Maiden Lane (shown below). Note the banners, announcing the "Norris Bros. Dog and Pony Show—Coming Soon," hanging from the shop. (AHS B109142, 13378.)

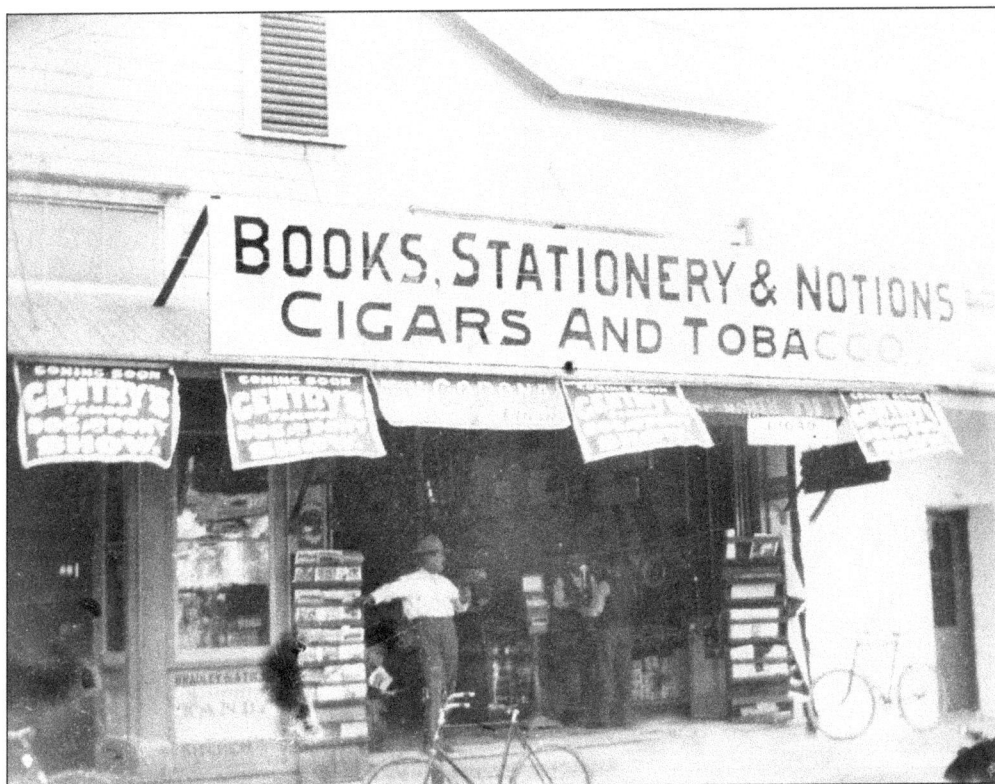

All manner of traveling troops, including circuses, thespian groups, and, especially, dog-and-pony shows, were keenly anticipated. The upcoming "Gentry's Famous Dog and Pony Show" was announced all over town (pictured above). The show arrived in October 1899 and paraded down Congress Street to the delight of residents, who lined the street (shown below). The Congress Lodging House at No. 60 is visible in background, as well as the roof of the Federico Ronstadt Company building at 41 Scott Street in the center at a distance. (AHS 13373, 13395.)

From the 1860s until its towers were added in 1881 and the rose window installation in 1883, making it a true cathedral, San Agustin was the spiritual heart of Tucson's Catholic community. A parade of O'odham riders gathered in the church plaza to celebrate the Reverend Peter Bourgade's elevation to Vicariate Apostolic in 1885. By 1897, venerable San Agustin was deemed outmoded and sold. In turn, it became a hotel, a seedier hotel, a bootlegging operation, a taxi stand, a garage, and was finally scheduled for demolition. In 1898 (pictured below), the once glorious cathedral was a hotel. (AHS B200330, 2472.)

Considered an eyesore and a magnet for unsavory activities, San Agustin was condemned until community leader George Chambers stepped in. Chambers convinced the owners to let him remove the famous stone facade and rose window, thereby preserving a vital piece of Tucson's history. Stonemasons disassembled the facade in 1936 (seen above). Chambers later donated it to the Arizona Historical Society, where this magnificent architectural feature has adorned the museum's East Second Street entrance since 1973 (pictured below). (AHS 102306, 102305.)

The 19th century closed with Tucson's impassioned espousal of Cuban independence. Responding to an explosion on the battleship USS *Maine* on February 15, 1898, that killed 268 crew members, newspapers of the day confirmed that every able-bodied man was ready to enlist in support of Cuban freedom. Before their departure to Cuba by special train, Tucson volunteers posed in front of the Orndorff Hotel in May 1898. (AHS 22676.)

Tucson firefighters championed Cuba's independence from Spain in the Fourth of July 1898 or 1899 parade. Actions of the Arizona Rough Riders brought national attention to the Arizona Territory, encouraging its citizens to believe that chances for statehood were increased. The "star" on the banner refers to adding another star, that is, the state of Arizona to the American flag. (AHS 13363.)

Four

COMING OF AGE

Tucson relinquished its frontier status (except as a means of enticing visitors to an imagined Old West), becoming a true city between 1900 and 1929. Technological innovations that began with the railroad continued with the automobile and the airplane. Improved transportation and communication consolidated Tucson's connection with the wider world, creating new markets and an influx of people who worked in department stores, at the university, in schools and hospitals, or established their own enterprises. Tucson's population in 1900 was less than 13,000, but by 1929, it had grown to more than 35,000.

Visually, the cityscape was reshaped as substantial stone buildings superseded low, linear, flat-roofed adobes. Tucson and Arizona matured with statehood as the territory became a bona fide member of the Union on February 14, 1912. Municipal services such as water and electric utilities, a gasworks, street paving, and public transportation added to the community's quality of life. The automobile and streetcar expanded residential neighborhoods beyond the immediate vicinity of the business district. Indeed, in less than two decades, equine-powered transport gave way to motorized vehicles, forever changing Tucson's ambiance.

While civic leaders continued to improve the city's social, educational, cultural, and economic institutions, the tourism industry became a foremost topic of conversation. Promoting Tucson—selling its mild climate, healthy clean air, and the West—was the sole goal of the Tucson Sunshine Climate Club, with the result that dude ranches, the Rodeo, automobile camps, fine hotels, and medical clinics proliferated. Prosperity was tangibly conspicuous in the fine new train depot at the beginning of the century and Tucson's two skyscrapers, the Pioneer Hotel and Consolidated Bank Building, completed in 1929. Yet even with the human tendency to view the past through tinted spectacles, the first two decades of the 20th century were not entirely rosy. The community was tempered by another war, and its successes gave rise to new problems as the river was depleted, groundwater reduced, and the hardship of a depression loomed. As it came of age, Tucson faced the challenges of a city.

Tucson's growing prosperity in the 20th century is clear from this bird's-eye view across business district rooftops looking west toward Sentinel Peak (left), Tumamoc Hill (center), and Congress Street (right). Substantial stone and brick buildings dominate the cityscape, c. 1912. The elegant El Paso and Southwestern passenger depot and park (farthest structure on left) had just been completed. (AHS B93483.)

Perhaps no single individual changed the look of Tucson buildings more than Quintas Monier, founder of Tucson's Pressed Brick Company. By 1900, then known as Monier's Brick Yard, the business supplied thousands of bricks for commercial and private construction projects. Monier eventually sold his company. Albert Steinfeld owned it during the 1920s and M. M. Sundt during the 1940s. (AHS B92789.)

The Southern Pacific Railroad rumbled into a wooden depot in 1880, but by the turn of the 20th century, Tucson mayor Levi Manning lobbied for a new, more impressive depot to keep pace with the city's new cosmopolitanism. The second brick, mission-style depot, with its elegantly tiled roof and Maynard Dixon murals, was completed in 1907, meeting all expectations. Quintas Monier supplied the bricks. (AHS B38369.)

A progressive community not only boasted schools, churches, hospitals, and courts, but also demanded a public library. City fathers, particularly Mayor Charles Strauss, took advantage of industrialist Andrew Carnegie's offer to grant funding for library construction. A successful petition resulted in the Carnegie Free Public Library, designed in the neoclassical style by architect Henry Trost. The library doors opened on South Sixth Avenue in 1901. (AHS MS1100 F19-G.)

The Southern Pacific Railroad broached the subject of building a hospital with Tucson archbishop John Baptist Salpointe out of concern for its employees. As more people converged on the city, it made sense to provide adequate health care for residents, and St. Mary's Hospital was born in 1880 with 12 beds. Tucson's first civilian hospital and sanatorium (pictured above), it was staffed by the Sisters of St. Joseph of Carondelet and, from its beginning, treated tubercular patients (shown below), many of whom sought or were prescribed a warm, dry climate. (AHS 24788-A, B38826.)

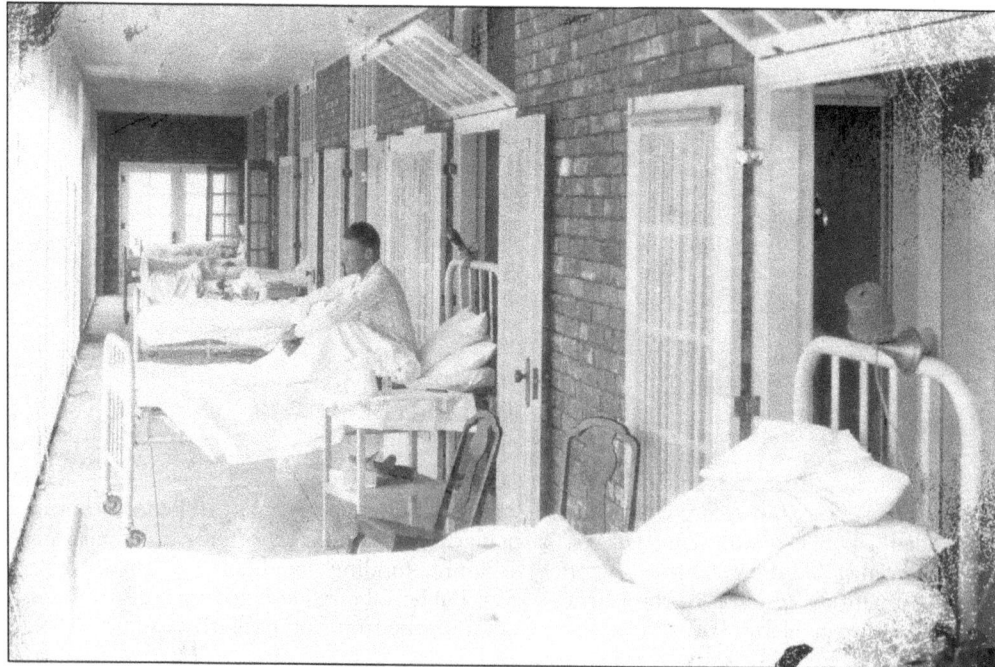

St. Joseph's Orphan's Home was founded in 1866 by the Sisters of St. Joseph of Carondelet to care for orphan and half-orphan children. The buildings (pictured above) were constructed on a site south of town in the vicinity of South Twelfth Avenue and Thirty-seventh Street in 1905. Destitute children from three to five years of age, regardless of color, race, creed, or nationality, were admitted and, if not adopted or claimed by relatives, lived out their childhood at the orphanage (shown below). Similar to the Tucson Indian Training School, girls were taught housekeeping and boys manual skills. Academic instruction emphasized English and reached an eighth-grade level. (AHS B93509, 62522.)

A fire department was established when the city adopted its charter in 1883. Funds were allocated, and the department's 1886 inventory included two hose carts, 1,000 feet of hose, and a hand-drawn hook and ladder truck. Although quick to respond, the lack of a pressurized city water system rendered effective firefighting relatively useless, as demonstrated by the

Radulovich disaster of 1898. Better equipped with personnel and gear, Tucson's fire department, shown here around 1905, depended on horse-drawn water wagons for the first decade of the 20th century. (AHS PC183-ME.)

Around 1910, Tucson's main business street remained unpaved, muddy after a rain as a city worker swept out ruts (and horse apples). Looking west on Congress Street, Tucson Hardware, Meyers and Bloom, R. J. Maghen—Books and Stationary, the onion-shaped dome of the Ivancovich building, and the Lyric Theater are on the right, with the Merchant's Bank and Trust and Craig Meats and Grocers on the left. (AHS B32948.)

The interior of Anton Grosetta's Tucson Hardware store, established in 1898 at 49 East Congress Street, helped supply the community's practical needs with small tools, paints, and sundries until 1929. A sign on the counter at left exhorts: "Turn Buckles. Does your screen door sag? Brace it up." The mustached Grosetta (right, c. 1905) stands behind the counter. (AHS 18260.)

Tucson businesses used photography to merchandize their stock with cabinet cards and, later, postcards, which were distributed to potential consumers. L. Z. and Company Hardware (c. 1900) advertises by way of a young woman, identified as a Miss Kennedy, wearing a costume festooned with spoons, chains, and a knife in her belt, while holding a rake to promote company products. (AHS B130.)

Three generations of Buehman photographers represent an uninterrupted chronicle of Tucson history, beginning with Henry in 1875, continuing with Albert after 1912, and ending with Remick around 1950. On his arrival, Henry Buehman, both a photographer and a dentist (a practice he later relinquished), first worked in and then bought out Juan Rodriguez's studio at Maiden Lane and Court Street. By 1881, Henry relocated the business to Congress Street, where he built a handsome building between Church Street and Stone Avenue. Showing business acumen, Henry established his Elite Studio on the second story while leasing the first to the Bank of Tucson, Wells Fargo and Company, and the Western Union Telegraph Company. The *Arizona Daily Citizen* offices, to whom he sold his photographs, was next door. Although later selling the building to L. M. Jacobs, Henry continued to lease the studio space, which remained a Tucson landmark for decades. The Buehmans photographed the people, land, streetscapes, and events of Tucson from its start as a village to its growth as a desert city. (AHS B200616.)

Photographer Henry Buehman's portraits cut across ethnic barriers. Two unidentified Chinese men, wearing a combination of eastern and western clothing, posed for a formal portrait at the Elite Studio, c. 1910. The Chinese came to the Arizona Territory as wage laborers to work in mines and on the railroad, but by 1878, state legislators had enacted laws prohibiting them from these jobs. In response to exclusionary laws, Chinese immigrants began businesses such as groceries, restaurants, laundries, and vegetable vending, and were employed as servants in the growing community. (AHS B112839.)

Henry Buehman was famous for costumed portraits. In full stage makeup with an eccentric wig, beard, glasses, and attired from neck to feet in peanuts, stood the "Peanut Man," c. 1910. Appealing and comical, the "Peanut Man," identified only as P. Beal, remains a mystery. Was he really P. Beal? Was Buehman actually P. Beal? Who was this man, and why was he covered in peanuts? No one knows. (AHS B5981A.)

After 1880, Tucson residents were increasingly anxious for Arizona statehood. Buehman created cabinet cards on patriotic themes to illustrate the territory's worthiness to be admitted to the Union. Here a man only identified as William Smith (c. 1907) was cast as Uncle Sam, possibly for a parade or theatrical performance. (AHS 14212.)

Gov. Conrad M. Zulick, in remarks to the 1889 Territorial Legislature, asserted, "the time has now arrived when Arizona should be . . . endowed with the duties and responsibilities of Statehood." It would take another 23 years to arrive. Above, the 1903 territorial legislators, joined by Sara Dugan Krentz (right), a page at the Arizona territorial capital in Prescott, enjoy a picnic of hardboiled eggs and lager, presumably to discuss statehood strategies. After more than 30 years of intense lobbying in Washington, D.C., Pres. William H. Taft (shown below) signed the statehood bill to admit Arizona into the Union on February 14, 1912. (AHS 60445, 17714.)

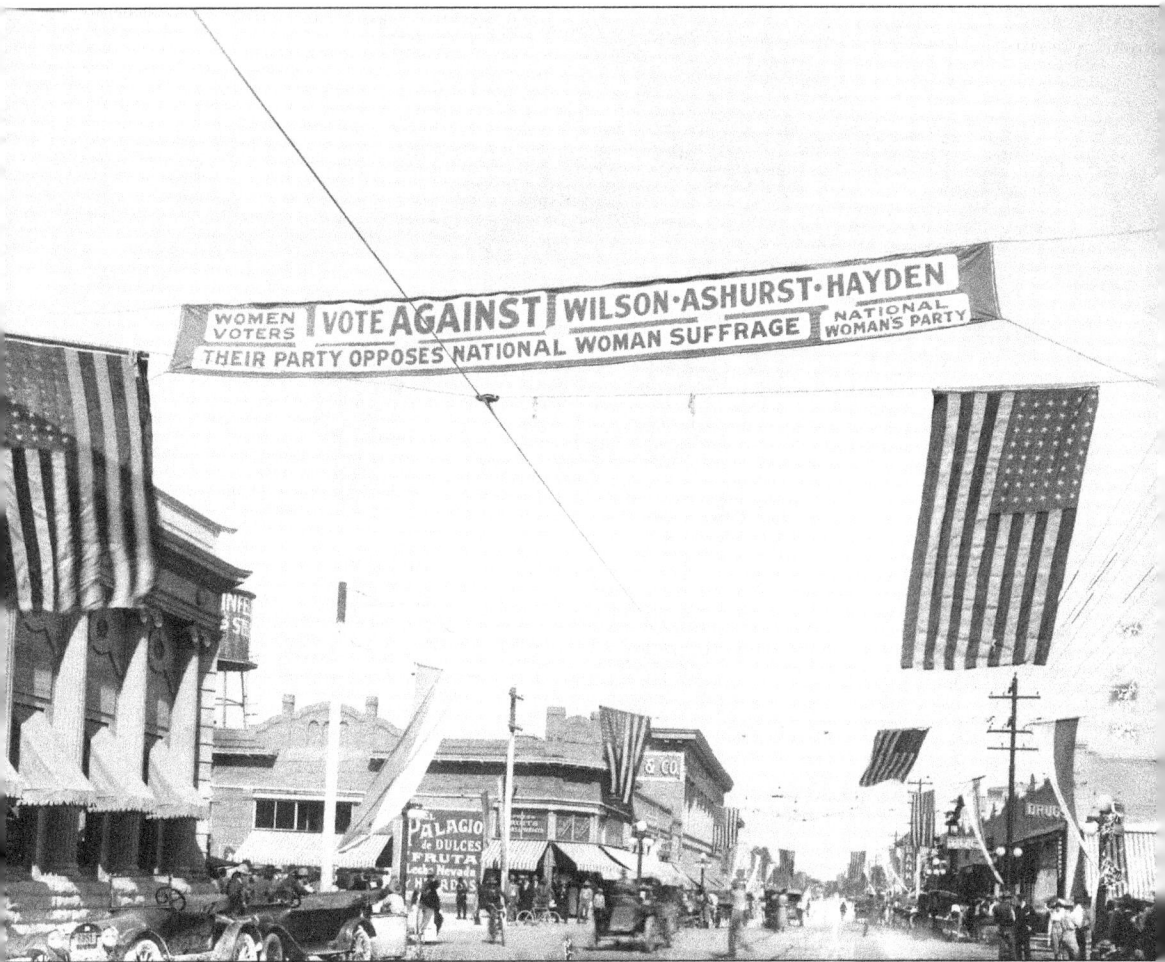

Albert Buehman captured the ire of Tucson women against Woodrow Wilson (for president), Henry Ashurst (for the Senate), and Carl Hayden (for the House) in the national elections of 1916, when these Democratic candidates failed to support national suffrage. Although Arizona women received the right to vote by referendum in 1912 state elections, it was not until 1920 that suffrage was extended to national elections. The banner across Stone Avenue made clear the position of suffrage proponents and the National Woman's Party. (AHS B32100-A.)

A scant five years after the euphoria of becoming a state, Arizona and the country entered World War I. Tucson fervently supported its "boys," as troops departed from the Southern Pacific Railroad Station on their way east, the French battlefields beyond, and finally welcoming them home. Tucsonans (pictured above, c. 1917) wait to greet troops. Troop trains passing en route to the European theater regularly stopped at the nearby Red Cross Canteen, where they received meals, coffee, and friendly conversation. Soldiers and sailors posed for a picture below, c. 1917. (AHS BN203774, B201050.)

Horses and mules that provided the principal mode of transportation were serviced by numerous local businesses such as Ortiz and Diaz, blacksmiths, farriers, and carriage builders located at 129 Congress Street and Arizona Avenue, c. 1905. William Flores Sr. is identified (center). With the appearance and eager acceptance of automobiles around 1900, the face of Tucson was rapidly transformed, and blacksmiths gave way to automobile mechanics. (AHS 64407.)

George Barry, an automobile mechanic, moved to Tucson in 1910 for his father's health. He drove "Big Ben," the Tucson Transfer Company's first automobile, photographed here in 1919. Early cars could cover much ground speedily, but Tucson's unpaved roads proved hard on fragile tires and set the stage for public paving projects beginning around 1910. (AHS 90450.)

Motorized public transportation greatly increased mobility and expanded the city between 1904 and 1924. Streetcars and taxis allowed people to live farther from their work places. The first taxi service connected Tucson with Nogales and offered competition to the railroad. Taxis from the Santa Rita Hotel (pictured above, *c.* 1918) served both visitors and locals. (AHS B32455.)

Barney Oldfield
Winner
103.142 Mi Race

Tucson's passionate embrace of automobiles was not just for practical reasons, but because aficionados loved speed. Licenses were issued in 1905, and a seven-mile-per-hour speed limit was enacted in 1903. A favorite pastime was to race down Speedway Boulevard (hence its name), a dirt track east of the university. Road races were also the rage. Barney Oldfield, driving a "Maxwell Special," trounced the field, including Eddie Rickenbacker, in this 1915 race at Steinfeld Track. (AHS 28883.)

Flight fever hit Tucson early. Charles Hamilton was given credit for the city's first flying demonstration in 1910. His airplane was assembled after arriving in parts by train and flown over a delighted crowd. Within days, Hamilton crashed and died in El Paso, Texas. Civic leader Sam Mansfeld (left), Vivian Ainsworth (later Mansfeld), and *Tucson Daily Citizen* editor O'Brien Moore (pictured *c.* 1906) posed on a flying contraption—lacking a motor—perhaps more indicative of promise than reality. (AHS 50201.)

After his historic solo transatlantic flight, Charles Lindbergh came to Tucson to dedicate the new municipal airport on September 23, 1927. Then the largest in the country, the airfield was named after Samuel Davis and Oscar Monthan, two pilots who died in the line of duty after World War I. Making several passes over the city in his *Spirit of St. Louis*, Lindbergh returned to the old airport on South Sixth Avenue near the present-day rodeo grounds to ecstatic well-wishers. (AHS B94401.)

Aviation pioneers included numerous adventuresome, dedicated women such as Louise Thaden, who received her private pilot certificate signed by Orville Wright in 1928. During the 1920s and 1930s, Thaden set endurance and altitude records, and won the first National Women's Air Derby, besting Amelia Earhart. Both helped found the Ninety-Nines, an international organization for women pilots. Seen here, Thaden landed in Tucson on one of her long-distance flights. (AHS BN341.)

Companies supporting a growing aeronautics industry formed as Tucson's airports expanded during the 1920s. Similar to the automobile industry a decade earlier, repairing, servicing, and fueling airplanes required new businesses. Arizona Aviation acquired the Curtiss Orioles (biplanes) distributorship and planned for flight instruction, passenger and freight transport, maintenance, storage, and sales. Sadly, the company was a little before its time and liquidated after only 18 months. Workers installed electric lights along South Sixth Avenue leading to the municipal airport, the site of today's rodeo grounds. (AHS PC183-MM.)

The Steinfeld stores (pictured above) long dominated the corner of Stone Avenue and Pennington Street. Established by Albert Steinfeld, who arrived in 1872 and bought out his uncle Louis Zeckendorf's business about 1900, Steinfeld's Department Store was heralded as the finest in Arizona. The downtown crowd could have a sandwich at the lunch counter and purchase their provisions in the Steinfeld grocery, declared by some to be the best in town. If tools and other supplies were needed, one could shop at Steinfeld's Hardware. Tucson's commercial landscape was also populated by more modest enterprises. For fun, residents could visit Oliver Drachman's Root Beer Stand (shown below), located adjacent to his fuel and supply business at North Fourth Avenue. Pictured around 1927, a lively crowd gathers for cold drinks, sandwiches, and ice cream at the first drive-in of its kind in Tucson. (AHS BN28077, BN22192.)

More cars, better roads, and promotion by the Sunshine Climate Club brought increased numbers of motorists, and Tucson tourism flourished. Mom-and-pop-owned automobile camps and motor courts mushroomed during the 1920s and 1930s, providing affordable lodging as an alternative to pricey hotels or dude ranches. Visitors could stay at Octa and Howard Jett's Auto Camp (above, c. 1923) at 2609 South Sixth Avenue in "clean cottages" and buy gasoline, food, batteries, or "good old Train Master" cigars in the grocery (below, c. 1936). (AHS 92699, 92698.)

Merchandizing, banking, mining, farming, transportation, and marketing the climate for health and recreation were all elements of early Tucson's economic strength. With the close of Apache hostilities in the 1880s, large-scale ranching came into its own. Edward Vail, famed as a cattleman, developed the Vail Ranch (pictured above, c. 1910) on the eastern slopes of the Santa Rita Mountains and, with his brother Walter, owned the Empire Ranch that stretched to the Mexican border. Ed deeded a right-of-way across his ranch to the Southern Pacific Railroad, who named a water stop Vail in his honor. When the railroad raised their shipping fees, Ed mounted a cattle drive to California instead; the Southern Pacific promptly reduced its rates, and cattle were again shipped by rail. Ed Vail was elected as president of the Arizona Pioneers Historical Society in 1926, forty-seven years after first coming to Tucson. (AHS BN201700.)

Reliable means of travel to and from a wider world, prospering businesses, and public transportation in town combined to create more amenities and services for the Tucson community. The Santa Rita Park pool on East Twenty-second Street (pictured above, c. 1925) cooled Tucson kids during the hot summers. The YMCA, another local favorite, provided children with after-school and summer programs, taught team sports, and gave swimming lessons. In 1928, boys (shown below) are taught batting skills, possibly preparing them for Little League or just learning to swat the ball. Interestingly, the El Paso and Southwestern Railroad offered to build Tucson's first YMCA in 1914 on the corner of Congress and Court Streets. The city was appreciative, and it was done. (AHS B22180, 10469.)

La Fiesta de los Vaqueros, or the Rodeo, is one of Tucson's most admired traditions. The idea came from Leighton Kramer, an avid winter visitor who wished others could experience the cowboy West during Tucson's mild months, when the rest of the country was deep in snow and gray skies. Kramer's scheme included a spectacular parade of horses, costumed riders, bands, and floats, culminating in competitive steer wrestling, calf roping, and bronco riding at the abandoned municipal airport. Kramer was the idea man, but the job of making the 1925 rodeo happen fell to Ben McKinney and Ed Echols; both of whom later became Pima County sheriffs. Above, the parade passes east along Congress Street, delighting throngs lining the sidewalks. Floats were a mainstay of the parade. Pictured below c. 1925, a determined pilot guides his bemused burro (a jenny) decked out as a Curtiss Jenny airplane. (AHS B110064, B92935.)

Sentinel Peak, located west of Tucson, was said to have been a lookout for raiding Apache by both the O'odham and Spanish. It became known locally as "A" Mountain after a University of Arizona football team defeated Pomona College. Cleared and trenched, basalt boulders were placed in the form of an "A" (70 feet by 108 feet) and whitewashed on March 4, 1916. The "A" has been visible ever since. It is seen here rising above rushing floodwaters of the Santa Cruz River around 1926. (AHS 62894.)

With increased settlement of the Santa Cruz Valley, the river suffered as woodcutting and over-grazing reduced vegetation, allowing surface run-off and floods. After the 1860s, dams, farming, gristmills, recreation, and well drilling contributed to an entrenched riverbed. The result was a lower water table that eventually eliminated a flowing stream and the familiar riparian habitats. (AHS 14503-B.)

94

Five

PROSPERITY AND WANT

Tucson during the Depression was a city of contrasts. A decade of boosterism, with leaders like Roy Drachman, Monte Mansfield, and Harold Steinfeld, marketed tourism through the Sunshine Climate Club, which publicized Tucson's fine hotels—the skyscraper Pioneer, the Arizona Inn, and El Conquistador—and increased the number of available rooms from 200 to 1,500 by 1930. Fancy dude ranches and exclusive private schools promoting a Western ambience catered to wealthy easterners. The decade opened with the glamorous launch of the Fox Theater. The municipal airport was completed, and Isabella Greenway was the first Arizona woman elected to Congress.

Yet hardship was near. Copper and cotton prices plummeted. Robberies became common. Small businesses and banks failed. Tax revenues decreased. Construction, farming, and mining jobs dried up. Tucsonans found it increasingly difficult to support their families. Disparity was obvious in the character of neighborhoods, the quality of schools, and huge crowds who availed themselves for economic help. The organized Charities of Tucson mobilized food drives to combat shortages, and civic leaders urged those who could to make jobs and hire local plumbers, mechanics, or carpenters. Federal assistance through departments of the Works Progress Administration provided much-needed jobs building the Sabino Canyon Dam and the Mount Lemmon highway.

Responsibility on the part of community leaders helped ease scarcity toward the end of the 1930s, with rekindled confidence as businesses began to recover and new jobs were created. Tremendous excitement greeted the construction of Old Tucson, probably the most famous Western movie set ever, the subsequent filming of *Arizona*, and the 1940 extravagant Hollywood opening. Optimism was combined with a growing sense that events in Europe would engulf Tucson and the nation. Preparedness became a dominant focus of city activities. Monte Mansfield served as chair of the Pima County Volunteers and Procurement Commission to stimulate enlistment. The municipal airport was converted and expanded into a military aviation center, and specialized jobs, including airplane mechanics, were in demand. Defense became a prevailing theme in Tucson celebrations and parades, such as the Rodeo. In 1941, an economically revitalized city was poised to confront the future.

The esteemed Santa Rita Hotel demonstrated just how far Tucson had come from the days of Phocion R. Way, who, in 1858, decried that there was "no tavern or other accommodation . . . in this God forsaken town." Built by Levi Manning and Epes Randolf in 1904 and photographed here around 1930, the hotel, located at Broadway Boulevard and Scott Street on what was once the site of Camp Lowell, represented a kind of formal, European elegance not previously found in the city. Its ornate lobby (shown below), roof garden, and public and private rooms, plus two orchestras, made the hotel one of Tucson's finest for many years. (AHS BN23503, PC174F12-A.)

The celebrated Pioneer Hotel was yet another symbol of Tucson's economic growth, even as the country moved into the Depression. Developed by Albert and Harold Steinfeld as one of Tucson's first skyscrapers, it had 11 stories. The other skyscraper was the 10-story Consolidated National Bank on Stone Avenue and Congress Street. The Pioneer Hotel was in the heart of the business district at the intersection of Pennington Street and Stone Avenue from its opening in 1929 until a devastating fire in 1970. During its heyday, the hotel was a part of downtown Tucson's bustle and excitement, including, on occasion, a fellow balancing on a wooden plank from the roof garden. (AHS BN202946.)

Located far from Tucson's downtown hum, near today's Broadway Boulevard and Country Club Road, the El Conquistador beckoned visitors for the quieter experience of an open desert, magnificent sunsets, and relaxation in spacious rooms, sun parlors, and promenades. Named by a contest sponsored by the *Arizona Daily Star*, the Sunshine Climate Club marketed the beautiful, sprawling resort, distributing many beautiful, appealing posters, c. 1930. (AHS MS970DR3F2-26.)

Architect Henry O. Jaastad blended Spanish and California mission–style architecture to create the El Conquistador (pictured above), which opened to great fanfare in 1929. Although the subject of much civic pride, the wonderful hotel was bankrupt by 1935. Following financial reorganization, the hotel continued to operate but never made a profit. As the city grew and slowly filled in the surrounding desert, El Conquistador met the wrecking ball in 1968, making way for El Con Mall (shown below). Architectural vestiges, including its copper dome and carved facade, can been seen around town today. (AHS BN203030, 44452.)

The Arizona Inn (pictured c. 1930), a still-thriving Tucson landmark, enticed visitors to enjoy a sophisticated elegance combined with a generous measure of Western informality. Frequented by the well-to-do throughout the Depression, it did not suffer the downturns of other establishments. Tucson architect Merritt Starkweather designed the inn for Isabella Greenway, Arizona's first Congresswoman. (AHS BN203023.)

Tucson became a mecca for guest ranches during the 1920s and 1930s, capitalizing on the frontier myth. Dudes could enjoy wide-open spaces under Western stars but without the hardships of true pioneers and with plenty of hot water. The Flying V (pictured c. 1940) was located at the base of the Catalina Mountains, west of Sabino Canyon. It started as a mining operation around 1900, became a working cattle ranch, and was a noted guest ranch in the 1920s. (AHS MS1255F494-5.)

The Western boots, jeans, and cowboy hat crowd fancied the rustic experience of guest ranches that offered trail rides, cattle drives, and cookouts. Flying V wranglers (pictured c. 1940) brew coffee and cook dinner in a Dutch oven over an open fire, with the chuck wagon full of provisions in the background. One cowboy strums a guitar while another rolls a smoke. Yes, it was a typical night on the range. (AHS MS1255F494-V.)

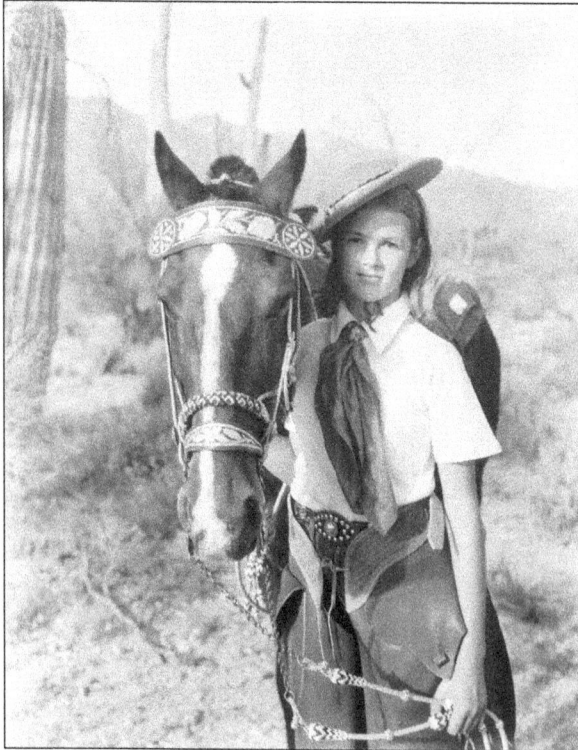

Increasing popularity for the West and Tucson's reputation for a clean, invigorating, and healthful environment gave rise to numerous private boarding schools during the 1920s and 1930s. Curricula were diverse, some emphasizing college preparatory courses, while others were more finishing schools, but physical education classes at most included horseback riding. The Arizona Desert School (pictured above) was located at the mouth of Pima Canyon. It was founded in 1927 for boys, grades 5 through 12. A student and her horse from the prominent Hacienda del Sol girls' school (shown below, c. 1930), both attired in fancy duds, clearly show the Western influence. (AHS BN22413, BN202327.)

Providing adequate education was a concern from Tucson's earliest days, and public high school classes go back into the 1880s. The classic building pictured above, recognized by generations of Tucsonans as Tucson High, was dedicated in 1924. A strategically parked ice cream truck waits for class dismissal during the 1930s. Support for schools offering specialized instruction, such as the Arizona School for the Deaf and Blind, was approved by the legislature's Enabling Act of 1910. Functioning as a department of the University of Arizona in 1912, the city donated 50 acres on Speedway Boulevard west of the Santa Cruz River in 1918, and the legislature privatized the school in 1929. Pictured below in the 1930s, a teacher supervises a model airplane project in a carpentry class. (AHS BN38769, BN202179.)

Tucson's highly regarded public and private schools educated many students, yet Pascua Yaqui children were taught in much less comfortable circumstances, with fewer supplies and instructed in a limited curriculum. Looking more like a class from the 1870s, Yaqui pupils (pictured above in 1928) pose by their school, a ramada-like structure, decorated with an American flag, which also doubled as a church. A note attached to the original photograph stated that an adobe building will be erected by Yaqui in the future. Masked *Chapayekas*, or soldiers, surround a Judas figure (on a burro) as they enact a stage of the Yaqui Easter ceremony in front of the church/ school below, *c.* 1930s. (AHS 29, 47212.)

Many early Tucson settlers, including Samuel Hughes, came as health seekers. By the 1920s, at least two dozen clinics, sanatoriums, and invalid boardinghouses treated respiratory patients. The Desert Sanatorium, which opened in 1926, specialized in tuberculosis. It was located in the desert against the backdrop of the Catalina Mountains, with the future Grant Road running east-and-west (pictured above from left to right, c. 1930). In 1944, it would become the Tucson Medical Center. The sanatorium's heliotherapy units (shown below) operated on the premise that controlled exposure to sunlight was efficacious in certain tubercular cases, although it was cautioned that sunbaths should only augment rest, good food, and fresh air. (AHS BN203572, BN203694.)

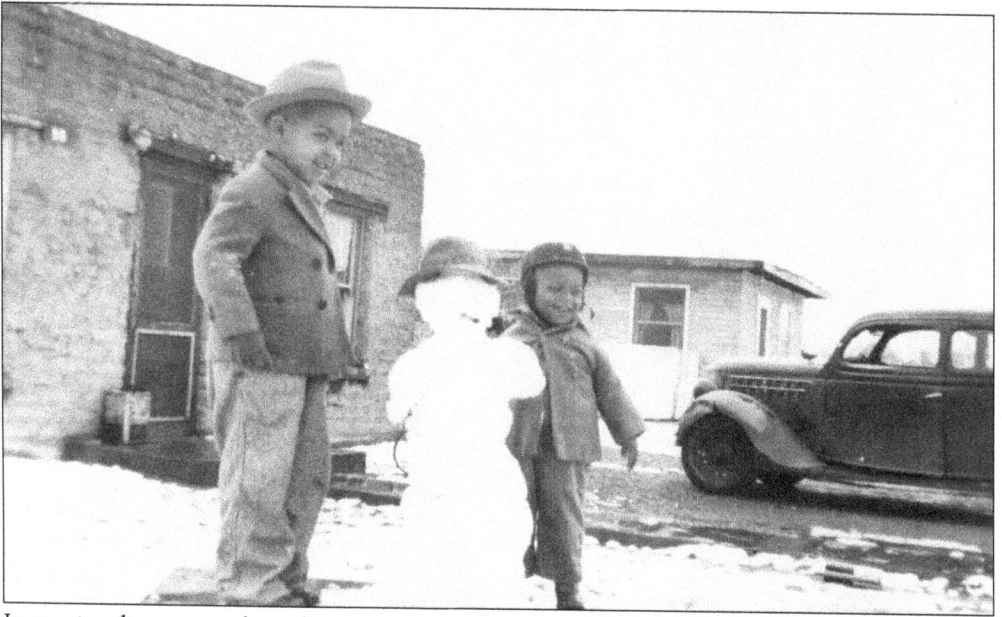

Increasing diversity, perhaps disparity, becomes more apparent as Tucson developed. The African American "A" Mountain neighborhood retained some of the "adobe" feel of early Tucson when 10 families lived there during the 1930s, and Charles Devereaux Sr., a cook with the Southern Pacific Railroad, moved into the neighborhood. His sons, Charles Jr. and Stanley, play in a rare Tucson snowfall (pictured above in the 1930s). No matter what the neighborhood, few Tucson streets were paved, and residents contended with mud or dust, depending on the season. Below, a 1931 Ford, a 1932 Chevrolet, and a 1935 Plymouth are parked on a rutted, dusty, residential street. (AHS 78370, BN33205.)

El Encanto Estates was once Tucson's posh neighborhood, where many city leaders lived in homes designed by well-known architects such as Merritt Starkweather, Henry Jaastad, and Josias Joesler. The home pictured above c. 1930, located at 45 North Camino Espanol, belonged to Benjamin McKinney, a pioneer cattleman, Pima County sheriff, and U.S. marshal. (AHS BN92831.)

Bungalow-style homes with shady porches and vented attics were architectural forms well adapted to Tucson's climate. Bungalows characterized many middle-class neighborhoods, especially those springing up around the university. The bungalow, located at 316 Speedway Boulevard and Fifth Avenue, was photographed around 1930 and survives today. (AHS BN204538.)

A tradition harking back to around 1905, Steinfeld's observed each season with a special window display. All were distinctive and often had a theme connected with city events or promotions and were awaited with great anticipation. The dramatic presentation, pictured above c. 1930, of Celanese (spelled Celenese in display) fabrics was accompanied with a banner declaring "Prints Fly the Airways of Spring." (AHS BN202767.)

Identified as the Rollins Motor Company in the Arizona Historical Society archives, automobiles were a big business in Tucson. The 1935 Hudson rumble seat coupe was photographed in front of the *Arizona Daily Star* offices. A cigarette advertisement in the window, showing a healthy young woman in a plain dress reads, "To knit and spin was not much fun. When twas my sole employment. But now I smoke these Chesterfields and find it real enjoyment." (AHS BN41300.)

If a Tucsonan frequented a department store, it would likely be Jacome's or Steinfeld's. Founded by Carlos Jacome in 1896 as La Bonanza, with the name changed to Jacome's in 1921, the store was a Tucson institution for almost a century. Seen here in the 1930s, Jacome's was at its Congress Street location. A civic leader, Carlos Jacome was a member of the 1910 Arizona Constitutional Convention prior to statehood. Tucson's business community included giants and smaller family-run operations. The Bring Funeral Home hearse (shown below) gasses up at the Union Oil Company station on Stone Avenue and Franklin Street in 1926 and, as was expected, received full, complimentary service. (AHS BN41256, BN200461.)

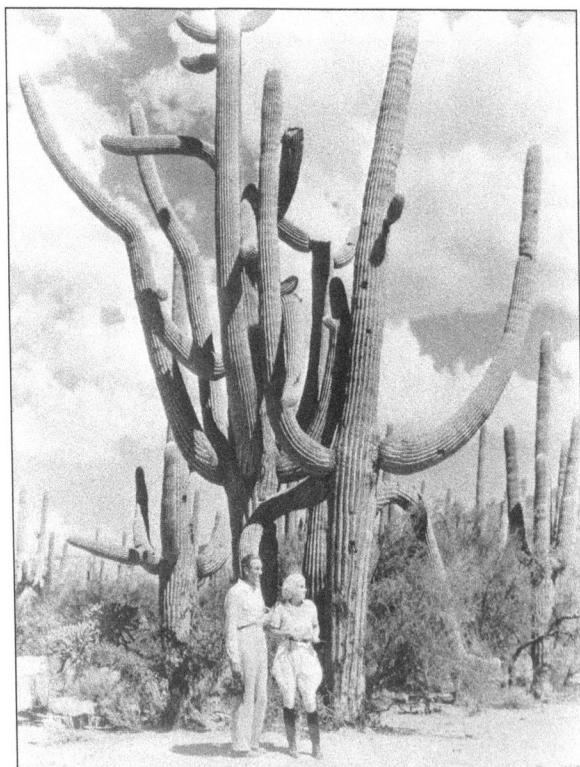

Tucson has a long history with moviemaking. Actor Dustin Farnum (pictured above) is shown being restrained in a scene from the 1918 silent film *The Light of the Western Stars*, based on Zane Grey's novel. The industry became more progressively active during the 1930s. During the 1933 filming of *Bombshell*, a camera-friendly Jean Harlow was photographed under an equally picturesque saguaro (shown at left). The plot of the movie has Harlow playing a parody of her own persona as starlet Lola Burns, in which she retreats to an Arizona dude ranch to find tranquility. (AHS BN308, B31846.)

Practically the entire town was pressed into action during the 1936 filming of *The Gay Desperado*. Streets were cordoned off, and Tucsonans were cast as extras (pictured above). Tucson's Police Department building (shown below) was altered to represent that of Mexico City, while members of the United Artists Company cast and crew pose for a picture. Actor Leo Carrillo is pictured in the center with a hat and bandoleer. (AHS 52275, B92987A.)

In an obvious come-what-may mood, the glitzy opening of the Fox Theater on April 11, 1930, marked the beginning of the Depression. Perhaps the most memorable Tucson event of the 1930s, as Diane Boyer wrote, bands played, there was dancing in the streets, lights blazed, movie stars appeared, and balloons and confetti rained. And, oh yes, a premier film, now forgotten, *Chasing Rainbows*, was shown. (AHS B35342.)

In its prime, the Fox Theater sponsored promotional competitions to attract audiences such as the Ladies Bicycle Race, won by Ann Daly on June 21, 1933 (pictured above). After the race, folks laughed at the antics of Al Jolson in the film *Hallelujah, I'm a Bum*. Tucson motorcycle police ensured crowd safety. Prior to a street event, officers were photographed at the Apache Tire Company, below, *c.* 1930. (AHS B27339, B41758.)

"Disney's Mickey Mouse Club" was arguably the Fox Theater's most popular program, attended by about 1,500 eager young people each Saturday. Members promised to be honorable, upstanding, and honest. Movies on Saturday, birthday parties, parades, and prize drawings, the Fox offered a place to have fun during hard times. Above, club members decorated their bicycles for a July 1930 parade. The club welcomed all. Saturday matinees were the only time the Fox was fully integrated; otherwise African Americans were restricted to the back balcony. Below c. 1932, happy contest winners held their Mickey Mouse doll prizes for the camera. Bert W. Wallis stands in the right foreground. (AHS B35336, B35325.)

Tucson's jobless rate skyrocketed during the early 1930s, so Pres. Franklin D. Roosevelt's federal aid programs were welcomed, putting some 1,250 Arizona men to work. The Emergency Relief Administration funded the 1937 dam construction in lower Sabino Canyon (pictured above), creating a favorite swimming and fishing locality (shown below). (AHS 16724, 17245.)

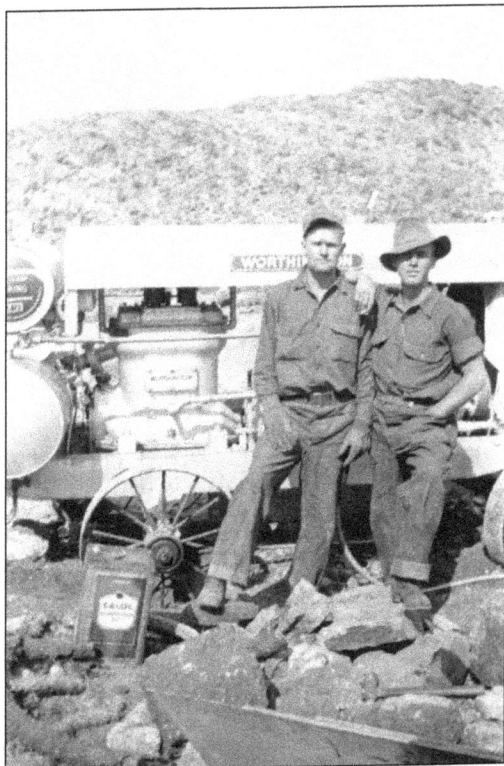

The Civilian Conservation Core was busy with numerous projects. At right, compressor operators E. Johnson (left) and Jimmy Banks pose on the site of the 1933–1934 Redington Road construction job. If jobs were not to be found, charitable agencies assisted Tucson's needy. The Salvation Army jackrabbit hunt, in front of a Stone Avenue church pictured in the early 1930s, was one means of providing food. (AHS 92364F2, B29259.)

Individual Tucsonans, including Albert (above, left) and his son Harold Steinfeld, stepped up to help Santa distribute presents during the holidays. Harold gave a free pair of shoes to every disadvantaged child and gift bags of useful merchandise to needy families. Below, members of the Mickey Mouse Club pose under a banner stating "The Lion and the Mouse—Contributions —to Keep the Wolf from the Door." The Christmas food drive was a function of the Lions Club and the Mickey Mouse Club in December 1930. (AHS 47308, B35324.)

Relief efforts were often centered on the Fox Theater. When *State Fair* played in February 1933 (pictured above), all proceeds from booths lining Congress Street in front of the Fox went to the Tucson Emergency Relief Committee, which distributed donations to various charities. On Bonanza Nite at the Fox (shown below), a patron's name was drawn from a hopper, and the lucky winner was allowed to select a bucket filled with sand. Using a small shovel, the contestant dug though the sand in search of a check or gift certificate. Not only did these promotions help the poor, but they kept the seats of the Fox filled. (AHS B24249, B27672.)

Anticipation mounted when Hollywood came to town not only to shoot another film, but to build a complete movie set 15 miles west of town that replicated Tucson of the 1860s (pictured at left). Desert and mountains provided the perfect setting for *Arizona*, a movie infused with pioneering spirit, Apache raids, scoundrels, and heroes. Starring Jean Arthur and William Holden, filming began in 1939 (shown below) and finished in 1940. Although the story line is pure fiction, historic Tucson and southern Arizona pioneer names like Solomon Warner, Pete Kitchen, Estevan Ochoa, and Sam Hughes were used with abandon. (AHS 51569, 51663.)

The *Arizona* crew and director Wesley Ruggles (above, left) relax between takes. Old Tucson modeled its set after Tucson's original walled presidio, including adobe and ramada structures from Spanish and Mexican days. Below, the set is shown as it appeared during filming in 1939–1940. Numerous Western movies and television features were filmed at Old Tucson until a devastating fire destroyed much of the set in 1995. (AHS 51652, 51631.)

Enthusiasm for the Rodeo Parade never waned. A large crowd turned out in 1941 (pictured above) to watch the Diamond Ranch float with musicians, horses, and riders as they passed the Santa Rita Hotel (left). The Greyhound Bus Terminal is visible (right, distance). Any activity connected with horses had many fans; Tucson was, after all, the real Old West. The world's first quarter horse speed trials were held at the Moltacqua Race Track (shown below) in 1941. The track was located north of the Tack Room, which was, for many years, a locally famous restaurant. (AHS PC177F18 1749, 14-9517.)

Music threads through the fabric of Tucson cultures and history, and is usually present at every festival, commemoration, event, or parade. Los Carlistas (pictured c. 1936) entertained throughout Barrio Viejo, in Mexican restaurants, bars, and on KGAR radio. The band members are, from left to right, Joe "Yuca" Salas, Soledad "Chole" Salas, Lalo Guerrero, and Gregorio "Goyo" Escalante. Born in Tucson, Lalo Guerrero, now considered the "Father of Chicano Music," was designated a National Folk Treasure by the Smithsonian Institution in 1980, was awarded the National Heritage Fellowship from the National Endowment for the Arts in 1992, and was given the National Medal of the Arts in 1997. Not bad for a Barrio Viejo kid who was born at home on Christmas Eve in 1916. (AHS 62647.)

The Depression years receded but an underlying unease pervaded the community as war in Europe escalated. The Girl Reserves of Drachman School (pictured above) and the Dunbar School drill team (shown below) expressed Tucson's patriotism at the Armistice Day parades of 1940 and 1941, respectively. The 15-by-23-foot flag was a citizen project created by fifth and sixth graders. (AHS 8507, 9461.)

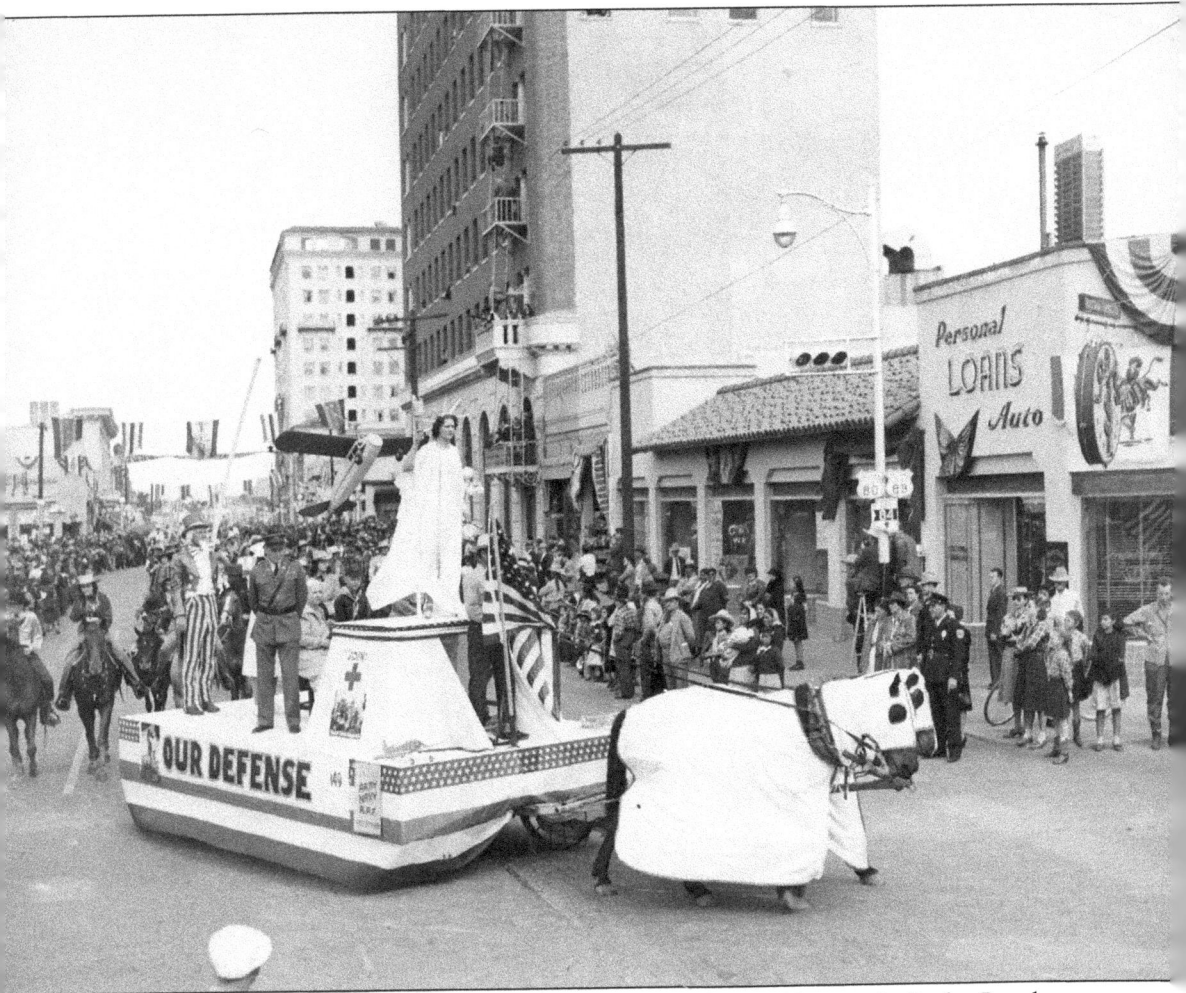

A harbinger of days ahead, Lady Liberty dominated a sober Red Cross Float in the Rodeo Parade on February 21, 1941. Lady Liberty is accompanied by Uncle Sam, a soldier in uniform, a Boy Scout, and a civilian carrying the Stars and Stripes. Model airplanes and posters decorated the float. One poster acknowledged the army, navy, and RAF (Royal Air Force). The other, by artist Samuel Cherry, refers to the Red Cross and urged citizens to "Join! Heed Their Appeal," speaking to the national defense theme. (AHS 15-9041.)

Neither the prehistoric inhabitants of the Santa Cruz River Valley, the Spanish garrison and priests who established the Tucson Presidio and mission, the Mexican soldiers who followed, or the Americans who first described the dusty little village with no amenities from atop Sentinel Peak would have recognized the city skyline of 1940. The early pioneers and visionary civic leaders who founded Tucson's businesses, schools, and churches, who struggled for territorial status and then statehood, would probably have marveled, perhaps shaken each other by the hand, and, with a sense of pride, looked down on what their enterprise had achieved. (AHS BN39758.)

BIBLIOGRAPHY

Bartlett, John Russell. *Personal Narrative of Explorations and Incidents in Texas, New Mexico, California, Sonora and Chihuahua 1850–1853.* New York: D. Appleton and Company, 1854.

Boyer, Diane. *Glitter Amidst Adobe: Tucson's Fox Theater.* Tucson, AZ: Journal of Arizona History, Arizona Historical Society, 29(3), 1988.

Browne, J. Ross. *Adventure in Apache Country: A Tour through Arizona and Sonora.* New York: Harper and Brothers, 1869.

Collins, Charles. *Apache Nightmare: The Battle at Cibecue Creek.* Norman, OK: University of Oklahoma Press, 1999.

Guerrero, Lalo, and Sherilyn Meece Mentes. *Lalo: My Life and Music.* Tucson, AZ: University of Arizona Press.

Henry, Bonnie. *Tucson Memories.* Tucson, AZ: *Arizona Daily Star,* 2006.

Kalt III, William D. *Tucson was a Railroad Town.* Mountlake Terrace, WA: VTD Rail Publishing, 2007.

Lyons, Bettina O'Neil. *Zeckendorfs and Steinfelds: Merchant Princes of the American Southwest.* Tucson, AZ: Arizona Historical Society, 2008.

Matson, Daniel S., and Bernard L. Fontana. *Friar Bringas Reports to the King: Methods of Indoctrination on the Frontier of New Spain 1796–97.* Tucson, AZ: University of Arizona Press, 1977.

Nequette, Anne M., and R. Brooks Jeffery. *A Guide to Tucson Architecture.* Tucson, AZ University of Arizona Press, 2002.

Sheridan, Thomas E. *Los Tucsonenses: The Mexican Community in Tucson 1854–1941.* Tucson, AZ: University of Arizona Press, 1986.

Sonnichsen, C. L. *Tucson: The Life and Times of an American City.* Norman, OK: University of Oklahoma Press, 1987.

Visit us at
arcadiapublishing.com